Fresh Ways with
Soups and Stews

COVER
Chunks of haddock and strips of sweet red pepper float in a nourishing broth that tallies only 125 calories per serving (page 71). The soup's base is a fish stock flavoured with wine, herbs and aromatic vegetables.

TIME-LIFE BOOKS

EUROPEAN EDITOR: Kit van Tulleken
Assistant European Editor: Gillian Moore
Design Director: Ed Skyner
Chief of Research: Vanessa Kramer
Chief Sub-Editor: Ilse Gray

Correspondents: Elisabeth Kraemer-Singh (Bonn); Maria Vincenza Aloisi, Josephine du Brusle (Paris); Ann Natanson (Rome).

HEALTHY HOME COOKING

SERIES DIRECTOR: Dale M. Brown
Deputy Editor: Barbara Fleming
Series Administrator: Elise Ritter Gibson
Designer: Herbert H. Quarmby
Picture Editor: Sally Collins
Photographer: Renée Comet
Text Editor: Allan Fallow
Editorial Assistant: Rebecca C. Christoffersen

Editorial Staff for *Fresh Ways with Soups & Stews:*
Book Manager: Jean Getlein
Assistant Picture Editor: Scarlet Cheng
Researcher/Writer: Barbara Sause
Writer: Margery A. duMond
Copy Co-ordinators: Elizabeth Graham, Norma Karlin
Picture Co-ordinator: Linda Yates
Photographer's Assistant: Rina M. Ganassa

European Edition:
Designer: Lynne Brown
Sub-Editor: Wendy Gibbons
Production Co-ordinator: Maureen Kelly
Production Assistant: Deborah Fulham

THE COOKS

ADAM DE VITO began his cooking apprenticeship when he was only 14. He has worked at Le Pavillon restaurant in Washington, D.C., taught with cookery author Madeleine Kamman, and conducted classes at L'Académie de Cuisine in Maryland.

HENRY GROSSI was awarded a Grand Diplôme at the École de Cuisine La Varenne in Paris. He then served as the school's assistant director and as its North American business and publications co-ordinator.

JOHN T. SHAFFER is a graduate of The Culinary Institute of America at Hyde Park, New York. He has had broad experience as a chef, including five years at The Four Seasons Hotel in Washington, D.C.

CONSULTANTS

CAROL CUTLER is the author of many cookery books. During the 12 years she lived in France, she studied at the Cordon Bleu and the École des Trois Gourmandes, as well as with private chefs. She is a member of the Cercle des Gourmettes and a charter member and past president of Les Dames d'Escoffier.

NORMA MACMILLAN has written several cookery books and edited many others. She has worked on various cookery publications, including *Grand Diplôme* and *Supercook*. She lives and works in London.

PAT ALBUREY is a home economist with a wide experience of preparing foods for photography, teaching cookery and creating recipes. She has been involved in a number of cookery books and was the studio consultant for the Time-Life series *The Good Cook*.

NUTRITION CONSULTANTS

JANET TENNEY has been involved in nutrition and consumer affairs since she received her master's degree in human nutrition from Columbia University. She is the manager for developing and implementing nutritional programmes for a major chain of supermarkets.

PATRICIA JUDD trained as a dietician and worked in hospital practice before returning to university to obtain her MSc and PhD degrees. For the last 10 years she has lectured in Nutrition and Dietetics at London University.

Nutritional analyses for *Fresh Ways with Soups & Stews* were derived from Practorcare's Nutriplanner System and other current data.

This volume is one of a series of illustrated cookery books that emphasizes the preparation of healthy dishes for today's weight-conscious, nutrition-minded eaters.

Fresh Ways with Soups and Stews

BY

THE EDITORS OF TIME-LIFE BOOKS

TIME-LIFE BOOKS/AMSTERDAM

Contents

1 *A Soup for All Settings* 13

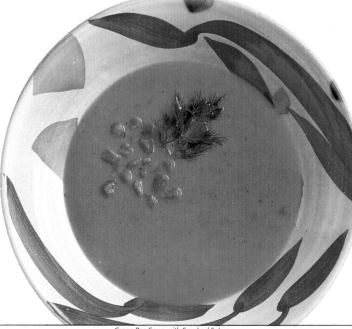

Green Pea Soup with Smoked Salmon

Mediterranean Fish Chowder

2 *Stew's Ever-Constant Magic* 89

3 *Microwaved Soups and Stews* .. 131

Sweet-and-Sour Fish Stew

...ck Stew with Watercress

Sustenance for Body and Soul

Soups and stews are time-honoured comfort foods, with rounded, blended flavours and soothing, sustaining warmth. Prepared more often than not in a single pot, they can incorporate all kinds of ingredients in combinations that are as nutritious as they are delicious. As the contents cook, tendrils of steam and aroma curl up, permeating the surroundings and inducing a sense of well-being. What dreary winter afternoon is not brightened by the companionable murmur of a simmering soup on the stove? What kitchen is not cheered by the rich scent of a bubbling beef stew?

Soups and stews have much in common, yet there is more to set them apart than the spoon or fork used to eat them. A soup can be thin or thick; it can range from a clear, light broth to a hearty chowder. A stew, on the other hand, possesses more body, and its components are likely to be chunkier. A soup can serve as a first course, a main course or — when made with fruit — even a dessert. It can also be a between-meal snack. A stew, however, often constitutes a meal in itself.

Stock, the basis of it all

What soups and stews share is their basic method of preparation. Both, of course, require a liquid — be it stock, wine or water — in which everything cooks. Indeed, a good, flavourful stock is at the core of most soup and stew-making. Recipes for five stocks — chicken, fish, vegetable, veal and brown — follow this introduction. Not least of their many benefits is the opportunity they present for economy; some of the ingredients — such as chicken bones and trimmings, which can be accumulated in the freezer — yield goodness that might otherwise have been squandered.

Stocks may be stored in the refrigerator for several days, or kept in the freezer for up to four months. (The exceptions are fish and vegetable stocks, which should be stored no longer than two months.) Once frozen, a stock may be removed from its container and tightly sealed in a polythene freezer bag, then labelled, dated, and returned to the freezer. Alternatively, it may be poured into a freezer bag fitted inside a container and removed when frozen.

Soups and stews are eminently practical. Almost anything edible can find its way into the pot, though the freshest ingredients produce the tastiest dishes. And because they cook in liquid that is consumed rather than discarded, soups and stews preserve most of the nutrients that escape from the ingredients themselves during cooking. Only a heat-sensitive vitamin like C is at risk here, and foods rich in it, such as broccoli, green peppers and Brussels sprouts, ideally should be added towards the end.

Besides offering sound nourishment, the 117 soups and stews in this book boast reduced levels of sodium, fat and cholesterol. The stocks specified in the recipes are all unsalted, freeing the cook to use a small amount of salt later, when it can most effec-tively contribute its flavour. Many of the dishes are degreased; a box on page 55 describes several methods for doing so. Where egg yolks, cream or flour may traditionally have been employed as thickening agents, vegetable purées are often incorporated instead, contributing the requisite smoothness and body.

Soups in themselves can play a role in weight control. They take some time to eat, especially when they are served piping hot, and they can be pleasantly filling. Moreover, the lighter, thinner ones possess fewer calories per mouthful than most other dishes, yet they offer just as much satisfaction. All this adds up to an unex-pected bonus. Scientists tell us that hunger is at least partially in our heads: the brain, they say, receives a signal when the body needs nourishment; it receives another signal as soon as that need has been met. As anyone with an appetite knows, it is all too easy to wolf down food. But when we start a meal with a hot soup, taking it in slowly as we must — spoonful by spoonful — our brain receives the message that our appetite has been curbed before we can overindulge.

In addition to their health advantages, soups and stews qualify as convenience dishes — and not just because they normally cook in one pot. Often they demand little effort beyond the initial prep-aration of the ingredients, and little watching. And because most cook slowly — particularly stews — tough cuts of meat respond by turning tender. Tomatoes or wine introduce acids that further help break down tissue. The liquid must never be allowed to boil rapidly, though, for high heat can dry out meat and make it stringy. Be particularly careful to cook such white meats as chicken and veal at a simmer; seafood, if it is not to toughen, should be cooked for as little time as possible.

The preferred vessel for cooking soups and stews is a heavy-bottomed saucepan or fireproof casserole, with even heat distribu-tion and enough capacity to hold the soup or stew without spillage. For six portions, a 4 litre (7 pint) pan will do. Where appropriate, use the lid to regulate the temperature of the mixture as it cooks. And bear in mind that certain metals, among them iron and aluminium, react with the acids in foods, or in wine and vinegar, causing dis-coloration and bitterness. A non-reactive pan, made of stainless steel or coated with such a substance as enamel, prevents this.

For making stock, a stockpot is ideal. The tall sides encourage the stock to circulate, allowing the heated liquid to rise to the top and displace the cooler liquid there. The pot's tubular shape also makes for a small surface area, ensuring controlled evaporation during the long simmering that is essential to most good stocks.

Fortunately, the preparation of stocks, soups and stews re-quires no other specialized equipment. Puréeing can be accom-plished with a sieve and the back of a wooden spoon, with an old-fashioned food mill, or with a blender or food processor. Each of the electric appliances has its special applications; the blender,

The Key to Better Eating

Healthy Home Cooking addresses the concerns of today's weight-conscious, health-minded cooks with recipes that take into account guidelines set by nutritionists. The secret of eating well, of course, has to do with maintaining a balance of foods in the diet. The recipes thus should be used thoughtfully, in the context of a day's eating, and not just with regard to the meal being prepared. To make the choice easier, this book presents an analysis of nutrients in a single serving of each soup or stew recipe, as on the right. Approximate counts for calories, protein, cholesterol, total fat, saturated fat and sodium are given.

Interpreting the chart

The chart below gives dietary guidelines for healthy men, women and children. Recommended figures vary from country to country, but the principles are the same everywhere. Here, the average daily amounts of calories and protein are from a report by the U.K. Department of Health and Social Security; the maximum advisable daily intake of fat is based on guidelines given by the National Advisory Committee on Nutrition Education (NACNE); those for cholesterol and sodium are based on upper limits suggested by the World Health Organization.

The volumes in the Healthy Home Cooking series do not purport to be diet books, nor do they focus on health foods. Rather, the books express a commonsense approach to cooking that uses salt, sugar, cream, butter and oil in moderation while employing other ingredients that also contribute flavour and satisfaction. Herbs, spices and aromatic vegetables, as well as fruits, peels, juices, wines and vinegars are all used towards this end. The portions themselves are modest in size.

The recipes make few unusual demands. Naturally they call for fresh ingredients, offering substitutes when these are unavailable. (Only the original ingredient is calculated in the ingredient analysis, however.) Most of the ingredients can be found in any

---

Calories **180**
Protein **21g**
Cholesterol **65mg**
Total fat **8g**
Saturated fat **4g**
Sodium **230mg**

---

well-stocked supermarket; the occasional exceptions can usually be bought in speciality or ethnic shops.

A glossary on pages 140 and 141 describes and defines any unusual ingredients. In instances where particular techniques may be unfamiliar to the cook, photographs and instructions explain them.

In Healthy Home Cooking's test kitchens, heavy-bottomed pots and pans are used to guard against burning the food whenever a small amount of oil is used and where there is the possible danger of the food adhering to the hot surface, but non-stick pans can be utilized as well.

Both safflower oil and pure olive oil are favoured by the cooks for sautéing. Safflower oil was chosen because it is the most highly polyunsaturated vegetable fat

available in supermarkets, and polyunsaturated fats reduce blood cholesterol. Where flavour is important, virgin olive oil is used because it has a fine fruity taste that is lacking in the pure grade. In addition, it is — like all olive oil — high in monounsaturated fats, which are thought not to increase blood cholesterol.

About cooking times

To help the cook plan ahead, Healthy Home Cooking takes time into account in its recipes. While recognizing that everyone cooks at a different speed, and that stoves and ovens differ somewhat in their temperatures, the series provides approximate "working" and "total" times for every dish. Working time stands for the minutes actively spent on preparation; total time includes unattended cooking time, as well as time devoted to marinating, steeping or soaking ingredients. Since the recipes emphasize fresh foods, they may take a bit longer to prepare than "quick and easy" dishes that call for canned or packaged products, but the payoff in flavour, and often in nutrition, should compensate for the little extra time involved.

Recommended Dietary Guidelines

		Average Daily Intake		Maximum Daily Intake			
		CALORIES	PROTEIN grams	CHOLESTEROL milligrams	TOTAL FAT grams	SATURATED FAT grams	SODIUM milligrams
Females	7-8	1900	47	300	80	32	2000*
	9-11	2050	51	300	77	35	2000
	12-17	2150	53	300	81	36	2000
	18-54	2150	54	300	81	36	2000
	54-74	1900	47	300	72	32	2000
Males	7-8	1980	49	300	80	33	2000
	9-11	2280	57	300	77	38	2000
	12-14	2640	66	300	99	44	2000
	15-17	2880	72	300	108	48	2000
	18-34	2900	72	300	109	48	2000
	35-64	2750	69	300	104	35	2000
	65-74	2400	60	300	91	40	2000

*(or 5g salt)

for example, yields a more homogenized purée *(box, page 20)*. The recipes in this book offer the cook choices, but the device considered best for the job is always listed first.

Many soups and stews can be prepared in advance. To inhibit bacterial growth, they should be refrigerated, partially covered, within half an hour. One of stew's endearing qualities is that it often tastes better the next day, when flavours have had a chance to mingle and blend still more. With a microwave oven, this trait becomes doubly attractive: a stew made ahead of time and stored overnight in the refrigerator will have deliciously matured, needing only brief reheating in the microwave.

Soups and stews can be stored in the freezer for as long as three months. But be careful: many seafood and vegetable soups do not freeze well — potatoes, for instance, turn mushy. And remember that soups and stews will lose some of their flavour and texture during the freezing process, and a little of their nutritive value when warmed. Thaw soups and stews gradually in the refrigerator, then gently reheat them.

How this book is organized

The recipes appearing in the first section of the book are all soups, and they are grouped according to their principal ingredient — vegetables, seafood, meat (including poultry) and fruit. Most are to be served hot, but many can be enjoyed cold. The second section is devoted to stews, likewise grouped according to main ingredient. The third section presents microwave recipes for both soups and stews.

The nutrient analysis accompanying each recipe is based on a single serving of the dish. For a soup that is to be consumed as a first course, the portion size can range from 17.5 to 30 cl (6 to 10 fl oz). As with all good menu planning, the cook should try to gauge how rich or lean the rest of the meal will be before selecting a first-course soup. For a soup that is intended as a main course, the serving size is naturally larger — 30 to 35 cl (10 to 12 fl oz).

Finishing touches

The cook's creative possibilities do not evaporate with the curling steam of a finished soup or stew. A main-course soup may require an accompaniment or a garnish such as croûtons *(box, right)* to round out its nutritional value or to enhance its visual appeal. Often, such low-fat accompaniments as water biscuits, crispbreads, melba toast, a chunk of crusty bread, or a slice of rye or pumpernickel will be enough to furnish the required starch. Similarly, nutritional balance may be achieved by eating a meat stew with bread, noodles or dumplings, accompanied by a salad or fresh vegetables. A vegetable stew may be served with a small helping

of meat or cheese, or a salad of beans or lentils, or followed by a milk dessert such as custard.

Where you can, match the type of bowl to the character of the soup, using delicate porcelain or glass for a clear consommé, say, and rustic pottery for stews. To hold the food at the appropriate temperature, warm the bowls for hot concoctions and chill them for cold ones. A tureen with a lid — the tureen gently heated with hot water before the soup or stew goes in — lends the dish presence at the table, acknowledging that food as good and sustaining as this deserves attention.

Finales with a Flourish

Home-made croûtons add the finishing touch to soup — and, when cut into fanciful shapes, they offer unlimited improvisation on the standard cube of bread. Because the croûtons are cooked without oil — the bread pieces are simply toasted in an oven or beneath a grill — they make healthy additions to whatever dish they adorn: smooth, creamy soups, chilled gazpacho, seafood soups or stews, even a hearty bean soup.

Use white bread or dark, but select a loaf for its fine texture. To make traditional croûtons, use a serrated knife to cut a slice of bread into strips 1 to 2.5 cm (½ to 1 inch) wide, then cut the strips crosswise into squares. For triangular croûtons, further cut each square in half on the diagonal. To produce the unusual profiles pictured above, use an aspic cutter. Arrange the pieces on a baking sheet and set them in a preheated 180°C (350°F or Mark 4) oven until they turn golden-brown *(above, lower tray)* — about 20 minutes.

To give new life to stale loaves of French bread, cut them into croûtes — small rounds of toast *(above, upper tray)*. For variation, slice each round in half and scoop out the centres, forming crescents, or simply cut the crust alone into rectangles or squares. Toast the croûtes under the grill, then float them in individual servings of soup. To add flavour along with the crunch, rub a peeled clove of garlic over each croûte.

Home-Made Stocks: Foundations of Flavour

A soup or stew is only as good as the stock on which it is built — and happily, making good stock is a simple procedure. The ingredients are simmered in a pot; when strained and degreased *(box, page 55)*, the cooking liquid becomes a savoury essence to serve on its own, store for later use, or elaborate into another dish. Recipes for five basic stocks appear on the right.

The elixir that is stock comes from humble beginnings indeed — inexpensive cuts of meat, fish bones, or chicken wings and backs. Attention to details will reward you with a rich and beautifully limpid stock: any large fat deposits should be trimmed away beforehand; large bones, if they are to cede the treasured gelatine that gives body to a stock, should be cracked first. During cooking, remove scum that collects occasionally on top of the liquid. Scum consists of protein particles released by meat and bones; these float to the surface, where they gather in a foam. As nutritious as it is, the foam must be removed lest it cloud the stock. Skim off the scum as it forms at the start of cooking; skim thereafter only as the recipe directs. After its initial rapid cooking, a stock must not be allowed to return to a full boil; the turbulence would muddy the liquid. As a final cleansing, the stock should be strained through a fine sieve or a colander lined with muslin.

To prepare stock for storage, divide it among containers surrounded with iced water. Wait until the stock has cooled to cover the vessels; otherwise, it may sour. Refrigerated in covered containers, any of these stocks will keep for up to three days. Because the fat on top of the stock will form a temporary seal, helping to keep it fresh, you need not degrease the stock until shortly before you are ready to use it. To prolong the life of a refrigerated stock, first remove and discard the congealed fat, then boil the stock for 5 minutes; either freeze the stock or boil it again every two or three days. As always, cool it quickly — and uncovered — before storing it once more.

Fish stock and vegetable stock may be frozen for two months; the other three may be frozen for as long as four months. Stock destined for the freezer must first be degreased; frozen fat can turn rancid.

The recipes that follow yield differing amounts of stock. Brown stock and veal stock, for example, are made from large bones, which require more water for cooking. But like any stock, these two freeze well, meaning an abundance is never too much.

Vegetable Stock

Makes about 2 litres (3½ pints)
Working time: about 25 minutes
Total time: about 1 hour and 30 minutes

4	sticks celery with leaves, cut into 2.5 cm (1 inch) pieces	4
4	carrots, scrubbed and cut into 2.5 cm (1 inch) pieces	4
4	large onions, coarsely chopped	4
3	large broccoli stems (optional), coarsely chopped	3
1	medium turnip, peeled and cut into 1 cm (½ inch) cubes	1
6	garlic cloves, crushed	6
30 g	parsley leaves and stems, coarsely chopped	1 oz
10	black peppercorns	10
4	fresh thyme sprigs, or 1 tsp dried thyme	4
2	bay leaves	2

Put the celery, carrots, onions, broccoli if you are using it, turnip, garlic, parsley and peppercorns into a heavy stockpot. Pour in enough cold water to cover the contents by about 5 cm (2 inches). Bring the liquid to the boil over medium heat, skimming off any scum that rises to the surface. When the liquid reaches the boil, stir in the thyme and the bay leaves. Reduce the heat and let the stock simmer undisturbed for 1 hour.

Strain the stock into a large bowl, pressing down lightly on the vegetables to extract all their liquid. Discard the vegetables.

Chicken Stock

Makes about 2 litres (3½ pints)
Working time: about 20 minutes
Total time: about 3 hours

2 to 2.5 kg	uncooked chicken trimmings and bones (preferably wings, necks and backs), the bones cracked with a heavy knife	4 to 5 lb
2	carrots, cut into 1 cm (½ inch) thick rounds	2
2	sticks celery, cut into 2.5 cm (1 inch) pieces	2
2	large onions, cut in half, one half stuck with 2 cloves	2
2	fresh thyme sprigs, or ½ tsp dried thyme	2
1 or 2	bay leaves	1 or 2
10 to 15	parsley stalks	10 to 15
5	black peppercorns	5

Put the chicken trimmings and bones into a heavy stockpot; pour in enough water to cover them by about 5 cm (2 inches). Bring the liquid to the boil over medium heat, skimming off the scum that rises to the surface. Reduce the heat and simmer the liquid for 10 minutes, skimming and adding a little cold water to help precipitate the scum.

Add the vegetables, herbs and peppercorns, and submerge them in the liquid. If necessary, pour in enough additional water to cover the contents of the pot. Simmer the stock for 2 to 3 hours, skimming as necessary to remove the scum.

Strain the stock, discard the solids, and degrease the stock *(box, page 55)*.

EDITOR'S NOTE: *The chicken gizzard and heart may be added to the stock. Wings and necks — rich in* natural gelatine — produce a particularly gelatinous stock, ideal for sauces and jellied dishes.

Turkey, duck or goose stock may be prepared using the same basic recipe.

Veal Stock

Makes about 3 litres (5 pints)
Working time: about 30 minutes
Total time: about 4 hours and 30 minutes

1.5 kg	veal breast or shin meat, cut into 7.5 cm (3 inch) pieces	3 lb
1.5 kg	veal bones (preferably knuckles), cracked	3 lb
2	onions, quartered	2
2	sticks celery, sliced	2
1	carrot, sliced	1
8	black peppercorns	8
3	unpeeled garlic cloves (optional), crushed	3
1 tsp	fresh thyme, or ¼ tsp dried thyme	1 tsp
1	bay leaf	1

Fill a large pot half way with water. Bring the water to the boil, add the veal meat and bones, and blanch them for 2 minutes to clean them. Drain the meat and bones in a colander, discarding the liquid. Rinse the meat and bones under cold running water and return them to the pot.

Add the onions, celery, carrot, peppercorns, and garlic if you are using it. Pour in enough water to cover the contents of the pot by about 7.5 cm (3 inches), and bring the water to the boil over medium heat. Reduce the heat to maintain a simmer, and skim any impurities from the surface. Add the thyme and bay leaf, and simmer the stock very gently for 4 hours, skimming occasionally.

Strain the stock into a large bowl; allow the solids to drain thoroughly before discarding them. Degrease the stock (box, page 55).

EDITOR'S NOTE: Any combination of veal meat and bones may be used to make this stock; ideally, the meat and bones together should weigh about 3 kg (6 lb). Ask your butcher to crack the bones.

Brown Stock

Makes about 3 litres (5 pints)
Working time: about 40 minutes
Total time: about 5 hours and 30 minutes

1.5 kg	veal breast (or veal shin or beef shin meat), cut into 7.5 cm (3 inch) pieces	3 lb
1.5 kg	uncooked veal or beef bones, cracked	3 lb
2	onions, quartered	2
2	sticks celery, chopped	2
2	carrots, sliced	2
3	unpeeled garlic cloves, crushed	3
8	black peppercorns	8
3	cloves	3
2 tsp	fresh thyme, or ½ tsp dried thyme	2 tsp
1	bay leaf	1

Preheat the oven to 220°C (425°F or Mark 7). Place the meat, bones, onions, celery and carrots in a large roasting pan and roast them in the oven until they are well browned — about 1 hour.

Transfer the contents of the roasting pan to a large pot. Pour ½ litre (16 fl oz) of water into the roasting pan; with a spatula, scrape up the browned bits from the bottom of the pan. Pour the liquid into the pot.

Add the garlic, peppercorns and cloves. Pour in enough water to cover the contents of the pot by about 7.5 cm (3 inches). Bring the liquid to the boil, then reduce the heat to maintain a simmer and skim any impurities from the surface. Add the thyme and bay leaf, then simmer the stock very gently for 4 hours, skimming occasionally during the process.

Strain the stock; allow the solids to drain thoroughly into the stock before discarding them. Degrease the stock (box, page 55).

EDITOR'S NOTE: Thoroughly browning the meat, bones and vegetables should produce a stock with a rich mahogany colour. If your stock does not seem dark enough, cook 1 tablespoon of tomato paste in a small pan over medium heat, stirring constantly, until it darkens — about 3 minutes. Add this to the stock about 1 hour before the end of the cooking time.

Any combination of meat and bones may be used to make the stock; ideally, the meat and bones together should weigh about 3 kg (6 lb). Ask your butcher to crack the bones.

Fish Stock

Makes about 2 litres (3½ pints)
Working time: about 15 minutes
Total time: about 40 minutes

1 kg	lean-fish bones, fins and tails discarded, the bones rinsed thoroughly and cut into large pieces	2 lb
2	onions, thinly sliced	2
2	sticks celery, chopped	2
1	carrot, thinly sliced	1
½ litre	dry white wine	16 fl oz
2 tbsp	fresh lemon juice	2 tbsp
1	leek (optional), trimmed, split, washed thoroughly to remove all grit, and sliced	1
3	garlic cloves (optional), crushed	3
10	parsley stalks	10
4	fresh thyme sprigs, or 1 tsp dried thyme	4
1	bay leaf	1
5	black peppercorns	5

Put the fish bones, onions, celery, carrot, wine, lemon juice, 2 litres (3½ pints) of cold water, and the leek and garlic if you are using them, in a large, non-reactive stockpot. Bring the liquid to the boil over medium heat, then reduce the heat to maintain a strong simmer. Skim off all the scum that rises to the surface.

Add the parsley, thyme, bay leaf and peppercorns, and gently simmer the stock for 20 minutes more.

Strain the stock; allow the solids to drain thoroughly before discarding them. If necessary, degrease the stock (box, page 55).

EDITOR'S NOTE: Because the bones from oilier fish produce a strong flavour, be sure to use only the bones from lean fish. Sole, plaice, turbot and other flat fish are best. Do not include the fish skin; it could discolour the stock.

1 *Thinly sliced sautéed mushrooms float lightly in a sherry-enriched soup that contains just 140 calories per serving (recipe, page 18).*

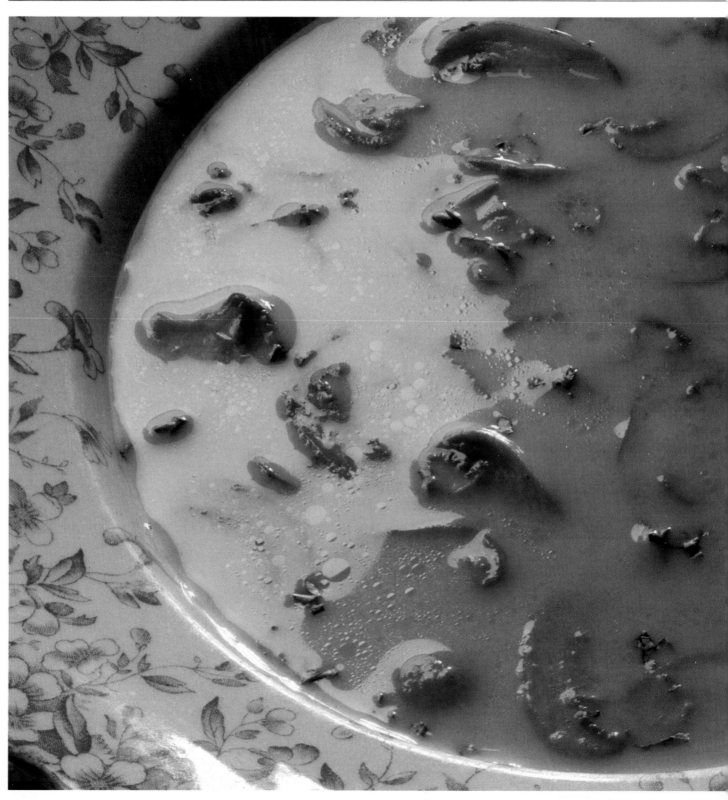

A Soup for All Settings

In the *grande cuisine* propounded at the turn of the century, one axiom was that soup should not be omitted from the evening meal. We are fortunate to live in an era of less exacting rules, when soup may appear at almost any time of day and in almost any position on the menu — from snack to main course, from appetizer to dessert. Indeed, soups may even constitute an entire meal. International restaurateur George Lang once had the audacity to serve his dinner guests a four-course meal of soups; he was chagrined to learn afterwards that a similar menu had been devised four centuries earlier — but in five courses.

This section offers soups of all types for all occasions. The majority are built upon one of the five stock recipes that appear on pages 10 and 11. But there are stockless soups too. Most of the recipes are simple to prepare, and some require only a minimum investment of time. The sweetcorn and coriander soup on page 33, for instance, is ready in 20 minutes. Similarly, Vietnamese crab and asparagus soup *(page 85)* takes only half an hour. And the cold avocado soup with fresh dill on page 19 can be prepared in 15 minutes; after an hour's chilling, it is ready to eat.

Many of the recipes were developed as updated versions of familiar concoctions. The beetroot soup on page 27, for example, is a fresh variation on borscht; to provide greater diversity of flavour and to subtract much of the fat and sodium found in the customary rendition, it includes lemon juice, parsnips and an apple. Caramelized shallot soup *(page 14)* presents a flavourful departure from the classic French onion soup; a splash of balsamic vinegar adds depth and greatly diminishes the amount of salt required. The peanut soup on page 41, meanwhile, contains only one quarter the fat of its American prototype; as a result it is a lighter version that satisfies without cloying. And the bread soup on page 17, while paying homage to the past and to one of the most venerable soups of all, cuts down on the oil and egg yolks that some consider essential to the dish; instead, flavour is built up by the inclusion of kale and chicken stock.

Caramelized Shallot Soup

Serves 4 as a first course
Working time: about 45 minutes
Total time: about 1 hour

Calories **190**
Protein **4g**
Cholesterol **10mg**
Total fat **7g**
Saturated fat **2g**
Sodium **245mg**

15 g	unsalted butter	½ oz
1 tbsp	safflower oil	1 tbsp
500 g	shallots, peeled and thinly sliced	1 lb
¼ tsp	salt	¼ tsp
	freshly ground black pepper	
12.5 cl	dry vermouth or dry white wine	4 fl oz
4 tbsp	balsamic vinegar, or 3 tbsp red wine vinegar mixed with 1 tsp honey	4 tbsp
2	garlic cloves, finely chopped	2
1 litre	unsalted veal stock, reduced to 60 cl (1 pint)	1¾ pints
1 tbsp	chopped fresh mint	1 tbsp

Heat the butter and oil together in a large, heavy saucepan over medium heat. Add the shallots, salt and some pepper. Cook the shallots, scraping the bottom of the pan often to prevent the shallots from burning, until they are caramelized — about 30 minutes.

Add the vermouth or white wine, the balsamic vinegar or wine vinegar and honey, and the garlic; cook for 2 minutes, scraping up the caramelized bits from the bottom of the pan. Pour in the stock and bring the liquid to a simmer. Reduce the heat and simmer the soup for 15 minutes. Stir in the mint before serving.

Black Bean, Bourbon and Bacon Soup

Serves 6
Working time: about 1 hour and 30 minutes
Total time: about 3 hours (includes soaking)

Calories **365**
Protein **24g**
Cholesterol **15mg**
Total fat **5g**
Saturated fat **1g**
Sodium **215mg**

500 g	dried black beans, picked over	1 lb
500 g	smoked bacon knuckle or forehocks	1 lb
500 g	onion, chopped	1 lb
5	garlic cloves, chopped	5
1½ tsp	dried thyme	1½ tsp
½ tsp	ground cumin	½ tsp
	freshly ground black pepper	
3 tbsp	soured cream	3 tbsp
6 tbsp	plain low-fat yogurt	6 tbsp
1	spring onion, trimmed and finely chopped	1
4 tbsp	bourbon	4 tbsp

Rinse the beans under cold running water, then put them into a large saucepan and pour in enough cold water to cover them by about 7.5 cm (3 inches). Discard any beans that float to the surface. Cover the pan, leaving the lid ajar, and slowly bring the liquid to the boil over medium-low heat. Boil the beans for 2 minutes, then turn off the heat and soak the beans, covered, for at least 1 hour. (Alternatively, soak the beans in cold water overnight.)

Place the bacon knuckle in a large, heavy saucepan. Pour in 3.5 litres (5½ pints) of water and bring it to the boil. Cook the bacon over high heat for 20 minutes, skimming off any impurities that collect on the surface.

Drain the beans and add them to the pan with the bacon. Return the mixture to the boil and cook it for 15 minutes more, stirring from time to time and skimming any foam from the surface.

Reduce the heat to medium. Add the onion, garlic, thyme, cumin and some freshly ground pepper. Simmer the soup, stirring occasionally and skimming any foam from the surface, until the beans are tender — 1½ to 2 hours.

While the beans are cooking, whisk together the soured cream, yogurt and chopped spring onion; set the mixture aside.

When the beans finish cooking, remove the soup from the heat. With tongs or a slotted spoon, take out the bacon and set aside to cool. When the bacon is cool enough to handle, separate the meat from the skin and bones by hand. Cut the meat into small pieces and return it to the soup; discard the skin and bones.

Whisk in the bourbon and bring the soup to the boil. Remove the pan from the heat and ladle the soup into bowls; garnish each portion with a dollop of the soured-cream-yogurt mixture.

Sweet Potato and Vegetable Soup

Serves 6 as a first course
Working time: about 45 minutes
Total time: about 2 hours

Calories **95**
Protein **4g**
Cholesterol **0mg**
Total fat **1g**
Saturated fat **0g**
Sodium **105mg**

2	large sweet potatoes (about 500 g/1 lb), scrubbed	2
600 g	cauliflower, cored and cut into florets, the core and leaves reserved	1¼ lb
3	onions (about 500 g/1 lb), 2 thinly sliced, the other cut into small chunks	3
1	whole garlic bulb, halved horizontally	1
250 g	courgettes, scrubbed, trimmed and cut into 2 cm (¾ inch) rounds	8 oz
1	lemon, juice only	1
	freshly ground black pepper	
1 tbsp	fresh thyme, or ¾ tsp dried thyme	1 tbsp
1 tsp	whole cloves	1 tsp
½ tsp	ground allspice	½ tsp
¼ tsp	salt	¼ tsp

Bake one of the sweet potatoes in a preheated 190°C (375°F or Mark 5) oven until it is quite soft — 50 minutes to 1 hour. (Alternatively, microwave the sweet potato on high for 7 minutes. Remove it from the oven, wrap it in aluminium foil, and let it stand for 10 minutes.) When the baked sweet potato is cool enough to handle, peel it and set it aside.

Meanwhile, peel the remaining sweet potato and cut it crosswise into thin slices. Set the slices aside. Cut the cauliflower core into chunks and set the chunks aside with the leaves.

Put the onion slices, cauliflower chunks and leaves (but not the florets), raw sweet potato slices, garlic, lemon juice and some pepper in a large, non-reactive pan. Pour in 2 litres (3½ pints) of water and bring the liquid to the boil. Reduce the heat and simmer the mixture; skim off any impurities that have collected on the surface. Add the thyme and cloves, and continue to simmer the liquid until it is reduced by half — about 40 minutes.

Strain the liquid through a fine sieve into a bowl, pushing down on the vegetables with a wooden spoon to extract all their juices. Return the strained liquid to the pan; discard the solids.

Purée the baked sweet potato in a food processor or blender along with 12.5 cl (4 fl oz) of the strained liquid. Whisk the purée into the liquid in the pan. Add the onion chunks, cauliflower florets, allspice, salt and some more pepper. Bring the liquid to a simmer over medium heat and cook it for 5 minutes. Add the courgette rounds and cook the soup until the courgettes are tender — 7 to 10 minutes more. Serve the soup either hot or cold.

Bread Soup

Serves 4
Working time: about 35 minutes
Total time: about 1 hour

Calories **275**
Protein **10g**
Cholesterol **6mg**
Total fat **11g**
Saturated fat **2g**
Sodium **605mg**

45 g	2.5 cm (1 inch) bread cubes, cut from day-old French bread	1½ oz
2 tbsp	olive oil	2 tbsp
1	large leek, trimmed, split, washed thoroughly to remove all grit, and thinly sliced	1
2	garlic cloves, finely chopped	2
1	small head chicory, trimmed, split lengthwise, and sliced crosswise	1
30 g	prosciutto (about 2 thin slices), julienned	1 oz
250 g	rocket or fresh kale, washed and stemmed	8 oz
1.5 litres	unsalted chicken or veal stock	2½ pints
2	potatoes, peeled and sliced	2
5	drops Tabasco sauce	5
½ tsp	salt	½ tsp
½ tsp	crushed black peppercorns	½ tsp

Preheat the oven to 180°C (350°F or Mark 4). Arrange the bread cubes in a single layer on a baking sheet and bake them until they are toasted — about 15 minutes.

Heat the oil in a large, heavy-bottomed saucepan over medium heat. Add the leek and cook it, stirring frequently, until it begins to brown — about 10 minutes. Stir in the garlic, chicory and prosciutto, and continue cooking, stirring occasionally, until the chicory softens — approximately 5 minutes. Add the rocket or kale and cover the pan; cook the mixture until the rocket or kale wilts — about 3 minutes more.

Stir in the stock, potatoes and Tabasco sauce. Reduce the heat, cover the pan and simmer the soup until the potatoes are tender — about 15 minutes.

Stir in the salt, pepper and toasted bread cubes; allow the bread cubes to soak up some of the broth before serving the soup.

Mushroom Soup with Sherry

Serves 4 as a first course
Working (and total) time: about 45 minutes

Calories **140**
Protein **5g**
Cholesterol **15mg**
Total fat **8g**
Saturated fat **3g**
Sodium **355mg**

7 g	unsalted butter	¼ oz
½ tbsp	safflower oil	½ tbsp
1	onion, thinly sliced	1
500 g	mushrooms, wiped clean, trimmed and thinly sliced	1 lb
1 litre	unsalted chicken stock	1¾ pints
4 tbsp	single cream	4 tbsp
4 tbsp	dry sherry	4 tbsp
½ tsp	salt	½ tsp
	freshly ground black pepper	
1 to 2 tbsp chopped fresh parsley		1 to 2 tbsp

Melt the butter with the oil in a large, heavy or non-stick frying pan over medium-high heat. Add the onion and sauté it, stirring often, for 4 minutes. Add the mushrooms, reduce the heat to medium, and cover the pan to help them release their moisture. Cook for 2 minutes, stirring several times.

Uncover the pan and increase the heat to medium high. Sauté the mushrooms and onions, stirring from time to time, until all of the moisture has evaporated — about 10 minutes. Continue sautéing, stirring the mixture frequently to prevent sticking, until the mushrooms and onions are golden-brown all over — 5 to 10 minutes more.

Transfer the mushroom mixture to a large sauce-pan; add the stock, sherry, salt and some pepper. Simmer the soup for 15 minutes. Stir in the cream and the parsley, and allow the soup to heat through before serving.

The soup is better reheated after a mellowing period in the refrigerator. It will keep refrigerated for as long as three days.

Dilly Avocado Soup

Serves 6
Working time: about 15 minutes
Total time: about 1 hour and 15 minutes (includes chilling)

Calories **110**
Protein **5g**
Cholesterol **5mg**
Total fat **7g**
Saturated fat **2g**
Sodium **165mg**

1	avocado, halved, peeled and cut into chunks, the stone reserved	1
½ litre	plain low-fat yogurt	16 fl oz
35 cl	unsalted chicken stock	12 fl oz
2	spring onions, trimmed and cut into 5 mm (¼ inch) lengths	2
1 tbsp	finely cut fresh dill, or ½ tbsp dried dill	1 tbsp
¼ tsp	dry mustard	¼ tsp
¼ tsp	salt	¼ tsp
	dill sprigs for garnish (optional)	

Put the avocado chunks, yogurt, stock, spring onions, dill, mustard and salt in a blender or food processor and purée the mixture until it is completely smooth. Transfer the soup to a non-reactive container (include the avocado stone, if you like — see note below) and tightly cover the container. Chill the soup in the refrigerator for at least 1 hour. If you wish, garnish each serving with a small sprig of dill.

EDITOR'S NOTE: *Because avocado darkens when exposed to air, cut it just before you purée the soup. The yogurt will help keep the soup from discolouring as it chills, but you may also want to try the Mexican trick of leaving the avocado stone in the soup until serving time.*

Curried Buttermilk and Courgette Soup

Serves 6 as a first course
Working time: about 30 minutes
Total time: about 1 hour

Calories **95**
Protein **3g**
Cholesterol **2mg**
Total fat **5g**
Saturated fat **1g**
Sodium **260mg**

1½ tbsp	safflower oil	1½ tbsp
1	small onion, chopped	1
2	garlic cloves, finely chopped	2
1½ tbsp	finely chopped fresh ginger root	1½ tbsp
½ tsp	ground coriander	½ tsp
½ tsp	ground cumin	½ tsp
½ tsp	turmeric	½ tsp
750 g	courgettes, thickly sliced	1½ lb
1	small apple, peeled, cored and sliced	1
¾ litre	unsalted chicken stock	1¼ pints
½ tsp	salt	½ tsp
1 tbsp	fresh lemon juice	1 tbsp
¼ litre	buttermilk	8 fl oz
1 tbsp	finely cut fresh chives	1 tbsp

Heat the oil in a large, heavy-bottomed saucepan over medium-high heat. Add the onion and sauté it, stirring often, until it is translucent — about 5 minutes. Stir in the garlic, ginger, coriander, cumin and turmeric; sauté the mixture, stirring constantly, for 1 minute. Add the courgettes and apple, and cook the mixture for 1 minute more. Pour in the stock and add the salt. Bring the mixture to the boil, then reduce the heat and simmer the soup, partially covered, for 30 minutes.

Purée the soup in several batches in a blender or food processor. Return the soup to the pan; whisk in the lemon juice and buttermilk. Cook the mixture over medium heat until it is heated through — 2 to 3 minutes. Garnish the soup with the chives before serving.

Leek, Celery and Gruyère Soup

Serves 4 as a first course
Working time: about 30 minutes
Total time: about 1 hour and 15 minutes

Calories **245**
Protein **13g**
Cholesterol **25mg**
Total fat **9g**
Saturated fat **5g**
Sodium **400mg**

1 litre	unsalted chicken stock	1¾ pint
1	leek, trimmed, all but 2.5 cm (1 inch) of the green tops discarded, split, washed thoroughly to remove all grit, and chopped	
7	sticks celery, chopped, several whole leaves reserved for garnish	
½ tsp	fresh lemon juice	½ ts
2	waxy potatoes, peeled and diced	
¼ tsp	salt	¼ ts
2	garlic cloves, peeled	
7 or 8	drops Tabasco sauce	7 or
½ tsp	white pepper	½ ts
12.5 cl	semi-skimmed milk	4 fl o
90 g	Gruyère cheese, grated	3 o

Heat 12.5 cl (4 fl oz) of the stock in a large, heavy bottomed saucepan over medium heat. Add the leek, chopped celery and lemon juice, and cook the mixture until the leek is translucent — about 5 minutes. Add the potatoes and cook the mixture for 7 minutes more, stirring often. Pour in the remaining stock, then add the salt and bring the liquid to the boil. Reduce the heat; add the garlic cloves and simmer the mixture partially covered, for 30 minutes.

Purée the soup in a blender, food processor or food mill, and return it to the pan. Add the Tabasco sauce and bring the soup to a simmer. Remove the pan from the heat and season the soup with the white pepper. Whisk in the milk and half of the cheese, stirring until the cheese is smoothly incorporated — about 2 minutes. Garnish the soup with the remaining cheese and the reserved celery leaves and serve immediately.

Puréeing: Why and How

Producing perfectly smooth soup — or a velvety base for stew — requires that ingredients be puréed. The means to this end are varied: where more than one method will do, the preferred one is given first.

For filtering fibrous particles from a dish made with such foods as celery or asparagus, a food mill works best; one with interchangeable plates offers a choice in the texture of the purée. Slower but still effective is the combination of sieve and spoon. Set a sieve over a bowl, then press small batches of the food through the wire mesh with the back of a wooden spoon.

For their speed and efficacy, the blender and food processor are clear favourites. Because the blender yields the smoother purée, such soups as gazpacho, where a coarse texture is the goal, are best prepared in the food processor. For the smoothest texture, purées formed with either device can be sieved.

Tomato Purée with Yogurt-Ricotta Stars

Serves 6 as a first course
Working time: about 25 minutes
Total time: about 45 minutes

Calories **95**
Protein **4g**
Cholesterol **5mg**
Total fat **4g**
Saturated fat **1g**
Sodium **155mg**

1 tbsp	virgin olive oil	1 tbsp
500 g	onions, chopped	1 lb
1	carrot, thinly sliced	1
1 tsp	fresh thyme, or ¼ tsp dried thyme	1 tsp
3	garlic cloves, chopped	3
	freshly ground black pepper	
800 g	canned tomatoes, seeded and coarsely chopped, with their juice	1¾ lb
30 cl	unsalted chicken or vegetable stock	½ pint
¼ tsp	salt	¼ tsp
90 g	low-fat ricotta cheese	3 oz
2 tbsp	plain low-fat yogurt	2 tbsp
60 g	watercress sprigs, stems trimmed	2 oz

Heat the oil in a large, heavy-bottomed saucepan over medium heat. Add the onions, carrot, thyme, garlic and some pepper, and cook the mixture, stirring it often, until the onions are translucent — 7 to 10 minutes. Add the tomatoes and their juice, the stock and the salt. Reduce the heat and simmer for 30 minutes.

While the soup is cooking, purée the cheese and yogurt together in a food processor, blender or food mill. Set the purée aside.

Now purée the soup in batches, processing each batch for about 1 minute. Return the puréed soup to the pan, bring it to a simmer over medium heat and add the watercress. Simmer the soup just long enough to wilt the watercress — about 1 minute — then ladle the soup into warmed serving bowls.

Gently spoon 1 heaped tablespoon of the ricotta-yogurt mixture into the middle of each bowl. With the tip of a knife, make a star pattern by pushing a little of the mixture out from the centre in several directions. Serve the soup at once.

Spring Onion Soup

COOKED SPRING ONIONS HAVE THE MILDNESS
AND SWEETNESS OF LEEKS.

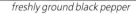

Serves 8 as a first course
Working time: about 15 minutes
Total time: about 50 minutes

Calories **75**
Protein **4g**
Cholesterol **2mg**
Total fat **3g**
Saturated fat **1g**
Sodium **150mg**

1 tbsp	virgin olive oil	1 tbsp
4	bunches spring onions, trimmed, white parts cut into 2.5 cm (1 inch) lengths, green parts sliced into 5 mm (¼ inch) pieces	4
2 litres	unsalted chicken stock	3½ pints
1	tarragon sprig, leaves stripped and chopped, stem reserved, or 2 tsp dried tarragon	1
¼ tsp	salt	¼ tsp
	freshly ground black pepper	

In a large, heavy-bottomed saucepan, heat the oil over medium-high heat. Add the white parts of the spring onions and sauté until soft — about 2 minutes. Pour in the stock and add the tarragon stem or 1 teaspoon of dried tarragon, the salt and some pepper. Reduce the heat and cook at a strong simmer, uncovered, for 30 minutes. Remove the tarragon stem, if using.

Add to the pan the tarragon leaves or the remaining teaspoon of dried tarragon, and the green parts of the spring onions. Cook the soup until the spring onion greens are tender — about 4 minutes more.

Tarragon-Courgette Soup

Serves 8 as a first course
Working time: about 50 minutes
Total time: about 1 hour and 10 minutes

Calories **110**
Protein **5g**
Cholesterol **7mg**
Total fat **5g**
Saturated fat **2g**
Sodium **230mg**

15 g	unsalted butter	½ oz
1 tbsp	safflower oil	1 tbsp
3	onions, chopped	3
750 g	courgettes, trimmed and cut into 2.5 cm (1 inch) pieces	1½ lb
2	carrots, thinly sliced	2
1.5 litres	unsalted chicken stock	2½ pints
1½ tbsp	finely chopped fresh tarragon, plus several tarragon stems tied in a bundle	1½ tbsp
¼ litre	semi-skimmed milk	8 fl oz
½ tsp	salt	½ tsp
	freshly ground black pepper	
	pinch of cayenne pepper	

Melt the butter with the safflower oil in a large, heavy-bottomed saucepan over medium heat. Add the onions and cook them, stirring often, until they are golden — 15 to 20 minutes. Add the courgettes, carrots, chicken stock and tarragon stems, and bring the mixture to the boil. Reduce the heat, cover the pan, and simmer the liquid for 15 minutes. Remove the lid, increase the heat, and boil the soup, skimming off any impurities that rise to the surface. Continue to cook, stirring occasionally, until the soup is reduced by about one third — 20 to 25 minutes.

Remove the pan from the heat and discard the bundle of tarragon stems. Pour the soup into a large bowl. Purée about two thirds of the soup in a blender or food processor. Return the purée to the pan. Briefly process the remaining third of the soup to achieve a coarse consistency, and pour it back into the pan. Stir in the milk, salt, black pepper and cayenne pepper. Reheat the soup gently without letting it come to the boil. Stir in the chopped tarragon. Serve the soup either warm or chilled.

Black-Eyed Pea and Spring Greens Soup

Serves 6
Working time: about 45 minutes
Total time: about 2 hours and 30 minutes
(includes soaking time)

190 g	dried black-eyed peas, picked over	7 oz
1 tbsp	safflower oil	1 tbsp
125 g	chopped onion	4 oz
30 g	mild back bacon, cut into 5 mm (¼ inch) dice	1 oz
1	garlic clove, finely chopped	1
1	bay leaf	1
¼ tsp	crushed hot red pepper flakes	¼ tsp
1.25 litres	unsalted brown or chicken stock	2 pints
250 g	spring greens, trimmed, washed and coarsely chopped	8 oz
1 tsp	salt	1 tsp
2 tsp	cider vinegar	2 tsp

Calories **130**
Protein **8g**
Cholesterol **5mg**
Total fat **5g**
Saturated fat **1g**
Sodium **500mg**

Rinse the peas under cold running water, then put them into a large, heavy pan and pour in enough cold water to cover them by about 7.5 cm (3 inches). Discard any peas that float to the surface. Cover the pan, leaving the lid ajar, and slowly bring the liquid to the boil over medium-low heat. Boil the peas for 2 minutes, then turn off the heat, cover the pan, and let the peas soak for at least 1 hour. (Alternatively, soak the peas in cold water overnight.)

Heat the oil in a large, heavy-bottomed saucepan over medium heat. Add the onion and sauté it, stirring occasionally, until it is translucent — about 4 minutes. Add the bacon and garlic, and cook them for 2 minutes, stirring frequently.

Drain the peas and add them to the pan along with the bay leaf, red pepper flakes and stock. Bring the liquid to the boil, then reduce the heat to maintain a simmer, and partially cover the pan. Cook the mixture for 40 minutes, stirring gently several times. Toss in the spring greens and the salt, and cook until the greens are soft and the peas are tender — about 10 minutes. Remove and discard the bay leaf. Stir in the vinegar and serve the soup immediately.

EDITOR'S NOTE: *Kale may be substituted for the spring greens.*

Green Pea Soup
with Smoked Salmon

Serves 4
Working time: about 20 minutes
Total time: about 1 hour and 20 minutes

1	leek, trimmed, split, thoroughly washed to remove all grit, and sliced	1
1	onion, sliced	1
1	carrot, sliced	1
1	stick celery, sliced	1
12	black peppercorns	12
½ tsp	dill seeds	½ tsp
300 g	frozen peas	10 oz
¼ litre	unsalted chicken stock	8 fl oz
60 g	smoked salmon, cut into small cubes	2 oz
2 tbsp	single cream	2 tbsp
2 tbsp	finely cut fresh dill	2 tbsp

Calories **245**
Protein **9g**
Cholesterol **10mg**
Total fat **3g**
Saturated fat **1g**
Sodium **160mg**

Pour 1 litre (1¾ pints) of water into a large pan; add the leek, onion, carrot, celery, peppercorns and dill seeds. Slowly bring the liquid to the boil, then reduce the heat, and simmer the vegetables for 1 hour. Add the peas, return the liquid to a simmer, and cook the vegetables for 3 minutes more.

Purée the contents of the pan in a blender, food processor or food mill. Rinse the pan and return the purée to it; stir in the chicken stock, the salmon and the cream. Bring the soup just to the boil; ladle it into individual soup bowls and garnish each portion with the dill. Serve immediately.

EDITOR'S NOTE: *This soup may be prepared a day in advance and refrigerated covered. If the soup thickens during refrigeration, stir in an additional ¼ litre (8 fl oz) of chicken stock before you reheat the soup.*

Beetroot and Parsnip Soup

Serves 8 as a first course
Working time: about 30 minutes
Total time: about 50 minutes

Calories **120**
Protein **3g**
Cholesterol **5mg**
Total fat **3g**
Saturated fat **2g**
Sodium **150mg**

½ litre	unsalted veal, vegetable or chicken stock	16 fl oz
500 g	beetroots, peeled and coarsely grated	1 lb
250 g	parsnips, peeled and coarsely grated	8 oz
2 tbsp	sugar	2 tbsp
1	large, ripe tomato, skinned and seeded	1
1	apple, peeled, quartered and cored	1
2 tbsp	fresh lemon juice	2 tbsp
2	large onions, finely chopped or grated	2
1 tbsp	red wine vinegar or white wine vinegar	1 tbsp
1 tbsp	finely cut fresh dill, or 1 tsp dried dill	1 tbsp
¼ tsp	salt	¼ tsp
	freshly ground black pepper	
12.5 cl	soured cream for garnish	4 fl oz

Pour the stock and ¾ litre (1¼ pints) of water into a large pan and bring the liquid to the boil. Add the beetroots, parsnips and sugar. Reduce the heat, partially cover the pan and simmer the mixture for 20 minutes.

Purée the tomato and the apple in a food processor or blender, then add the purée to the simmering soup. Add the lemon juice, onions and vinegar. Cover the pan and simmer the soup for 20 minutes more. Stir in the dill, salt and some pepper. Serve the soup piping hot, garnished with the soured cream.

Vegetable-Broth Minestrone

Serves 6
Working time: about 30 minutes
Total time: about 2 hours

Calories **305**
Protein **16g**
Cholesterol **0mg**
Total fat **2g**
Saturated fat **0g**
Sodium **205mg**

Metric	Ingredient	Imperial
190 g	dried pinto beans, picked over	7 oz
2	onions, unpeeled, halved crosswise	2
12.5 cl	dry white wine	4 fl oz
250 g	mushrooms, wiped clean, stems removed and reserved, the caps sliced	8 oz
500 g	ripe tomatoes, skinned, seeded and chopped, skins, seeds and juice reserved, or 400 g (14 oz) canned tomatoes, seeded and chopped, seeds and juice reserved	1 lb
2	carrots, sliced	2
2	sticks celery, sliced, leaves chopped	2
1	cauliflower, broken into florets, leaves and core coarsely chopped	1
2	broccoli stalks, florets broken off, leaves and stalks coarsely chopped	2
1	whole garlic bulb, unpeeled cloves separated and crushed with the side of a heavy knife, plus 4 garlic cloves, chopped	1
24	black peppercorns	24
1 tsp	fresh rosemary, or ¼ tsp dried rosemary	1 tsp
2	bay leaves	2
2	5 cm (2 inch) long strips of lemon rind	2
125 g	ziti or other tubular pasta	4 oz
½	lemon, juice only	½
¼ tsp	salt	¼ tsp
60 g	sliced fresh basil leaves, or 4 tbsp chopped fresh parsley	2 oz
	freshly ground black pepper	
60 g	Parmesan cheese, freshly grated	2 oz

Rinse the beans under cold running water. Put the beans into a large pan and pour in enough cold water to cover them by about 7.5 cm (3 inches). Discard any beans that float to the surface. Boil the beans for 2 minutes, then turn off the heat, cover the pan, and soak the beans for at least 1 hour. (Alternatively, soak the beans overnight in cold water.)

At the end of the soaking time, pour in enough additional water to cover the beans by about 7.5 cm (3 inches). Bring the liquid to the boil, reduce the heat to maintain a strong simmer, and cook the beans until they are tender — about 30 minutes. Then drain the beans and set them aside.

While the beans are simmering, start the vegetable broth. Heat a large, heavy-bottomed saucepan over medium-high heat and place the onions flat sides down in the pot. Cook the onions until their cut surfaces turn dark brown — about 10 minutes. (The onions will help to colour the stock.) Pour in the wine, stirring with a wooden spoon to dislodge the onions and dissolve their caramelized juices. Add the mushroom stems, the tomato skins, seeds and juice, half of the carrots, the sliced celery, the chopped cauliflower leaves and core, the chopped broccoli leaves and stalks, the crushed garlic cloves, peppercorns, rose-

mary, bay leaves, lemon rind and 3 litres (5 pints) of water. Bring the liquid to the boil, then reduce the heat to maintain a simmer and cook the broth for 1 hour.

While the both is simmering, add the ziti to 1.5 litres (2½ pints) of boiling water with 1 teaspoon of salt. Start testing the pasta after 8 minutes and cook it until it is *al dente*. Drain the pasta, rinse it under cold running water to keep it from sticking together, and set it aside.

In a small bowl, mix the chopped tomato and the chopped garlic with the lemon juice and salt, and set the mixture aside.

When the vegetable broth has simmered for 1 hour, strain it into a bowl and discard the solids. Rinse the pan and return the strained broth to it. Bring the broth to the boil. Reduce the heat to medium, then add the sliced mushroom caps and the remaining carrots, and simmer them for 4 minutes. Add the cauliflower florets and simmer them for 4 minutes more. Add the broccoli florets, celery leaves and beans, and simmer them for an additional 3 minutes.

Transfer the drained ziti to the pan and cook for 2 minutes to warm the pasta through. Stir in the tomato-garlic mixture and the basil or parsley. Season the minestrone with a generous grinding of pepper, and serve it with the grated cheese.

Gazpacho Blanco

Serves 4 as a first course
Working time: about 10 minutes
Total time: about 40 minutes

Calories **165**
Protein **7g**
Cholesterol **7mg**
Total fat **2g**
Saturated fat **1g**
Sodium **220mg**

500 g	seedless white grapes	1 lb
2	cucumbers (about 750 g/1 ½ lb)	2
1	shallot, sliced	1
1	small garlic clove, finely chopped	1
¼ tsp	salt	¼ tsp
¼ tsp	white pepper	¼ tsp
½ litre	plain low-fat yogurt	16 fl oz
5 to 8	drops Tabasco sauce	5 to 8

Wash and stem the grapes. Cut several of them in half lengthwise and set them aside. Purée the remaining grapes in a food processor or blender. Strain the purée through a sieve and return it to the food processor or blender.

Cut several very thin slices from the centre of one cucumber and set them aside. Peel the cucumbers, halve them lengthwise, and seed them. Cut the cucumbers into thick slices and add them to the grape purée in the processor or blender. Add the shallot, garlic, salt and pepper, and briefly process the mixture until the cucumbers are reduced to fine pieces.

Pour the mixture into a chilled serving bowl and whisk in the yogurt and Tabasco sauce. Cover the soup and refrigerate it until it is well chilled — about 30 minutes. Serve the soup in chilled bowls, garnished with the reserved cucumber slices and grape halves.

Onion and Red Potato Soup with Walnut Toasts

Serves 4 as a first course
Working (and total) time: about 30 minutes

Calories **220**
Protein **7g**
Cholesterol **2mg**
Total fat **9g**
Saturated fat **1g**
Sodium **290mg**

1 litre	unsalted chicken stock	1¾ pints
2	onions (about 300 g/10 oz), cut into eighths	2
250 g	red-skinned potatoes, unpeeled, cut into 2 cm (¾ inch) pieces	8 oz
¼ tsp	salt	¼ tsp
	freshly ground black pepper	
4	garlic cloves, finely chopped	4
4 tbsp	coarsely chopped walnuts, plus 4 large walnut halves	4 tbsp
4	slices French bread, each about 5 mm (¼ inch) thick	4
4 tbsp	thinly sliced fresh basil leaves	4 tbsp

Pour the stock into a large saucepan over medium heat. When the stock begins to steam, add the onions, potatoes, salt, some pepper and half of the garlic. Simmer the liquid until the potatoes can be easily pierced with a fork — 10 to 15 minutes.

While the potatoes are cooking, preheat the oven to 200°C (400°F or Mark 6). Using a mortar and pestle, crush 3 tablespoons of the walnuts with the remaining garlic to form a paste. Spread one quarter of the paste on each slice of bread, then press a walnut half into the centre of each slice. Toast the bread in the oven until the slices are slightly browned on the bottom — about 5 minutes.

Stir the basil into the soup and immediately ladle the soup into four heated bowls. Float a walnut-covered slice of bread in the centre of each bowl; sprinkle some of the remaining chopped walnuts around each slice and serve the soup immediately.

Cold Curried Vegetable Soup

Serves 4 as a first course
Working time: about 20 minutes
Total time: about 2 hours and 20 minutes
(includes chilling)

Calories **130**			
Protein **5g**	2 tsp	safflower oil	2 tsp
Cholesterol **1mg**	1	small onion, thinly sliced	1
Total fat **4g**	2 tbsp	mild curry powder	2 tbsp
Saturated fat **1g**	2	garlic cloves, finely chopped	2
Sodium **220mg**	400 g	canned tomatoes, coarsely chopped, with their juice	14 oz
	¾ litre	unsalted chicken stock	1¼ pints
	1 tsp	chopped fresh thyme, or ¼ tsp dried thyme	1 tsp
	1	sweet green pepper, seeded, deribbed and cut into 1 cm (½ inch) pieces	1
	90 g	cauliflower florets, thinly sliced lengthwise	3 oz
	1	small carrot, thinly sliced	1
	2	small courgettes (preferably 1 green, 1 yellow), thinly sliced	2
	1 tbsp	balsamic vinegar or red wine vinegar	1 tbsp
	¼ tsp	salt	¼ tsp
		freshly ground black pepper	

Heat the safflower oil in a large, heavy-bottomed saucepan over medium heat. Add the onion slices and sauté them, stirring, until they are translucent — about 4 minutes. Sprinkle in the curry powder and cook the mixture, stirring constantly, for 1 minute. Add the garlic and cook it for 30 seconds. Stir in the tomatoes with their juice and cook them, stirring frequently, until the liquid is reduced by about one third — 10 to 15 minutes.

While the tomatoes are cooking, pour the stock into a large pot over medium-high heat. Add the thyme and place a steamer in the pot. Arrange the green pepper, cauliflower, carrot and courgettes in the steamer. Cover the pot and steam the vegetables until they are tender — 5 to 7 minutes. Transfer the vegetables to the tomato mixture and pour in the steaming liquid. Add the vinegar, salt and some black pepper, then gently stir the soup to incorporate the vegetables. Refrigerate the soup, partially covered, for at least 2 hours before serving.

EDITOR'S NOTE: *This soup may be prepared as much as two days in advance.*

Cold Parsley Soup with Icy Tomato Granita

GRANITA IS THE ITALIAN NAME FOR A WATER ICE.
THE CRYSTALLINE TEXTURE OF THE TOMATO-MINT GRANITA
USED HERE PROVIDES A SUBTLE COUNTERPOINT TO THE
SOUP'S SMOOTHNESS.

Serves 6 as a first course
Working time: about 45 minutes
Total time: about 3 hours and 45 minutes
(includes chilling)

Calories **100**
Protein **4g**
Cholesterol **1mg**
Total fat **4g**
Saturated fat **1g**
Sodium **255mg**

1 tbsp	virgin olive oil	1 tbsp
4	spring onions, trimmed and thinly sliced	4
1	onion, thinly sliced	1
2	garlic cloves, finely chopped	2
¼ tsp	salt	¼ tsp
	freshly ground black pepper	
1 litre	unsalted chicken or vegetable stock	1¾ pints
1	potato, peeled and thinly sliced	1
125 g	parsley leaves, preferably flat-leaf	4 oz
6	mint sprigs for garnish	6
Tomato granita		
500 g	ripe tomatoes, skinned, cored and quartered	1 lb
¼ tsp	salt	¼ tsp
1 tbsp	fresh lemon juice	1 tbsp
2 tbsp	finely chopped fresh mint	2 tbsp

To prepare the granita, purée the tomatoes in a blender or food processor, then strain the purée through a sieve into a bowl. Stir in the salt, lemon juice and mint. Pour the mixture into ice-cube trays and freeze it for 2 to 3 hours.

Meanwhile, heat the oil in a large, heavy-bottomed saucepan over medium heat. Add the spring onions, onion, garlic, salt and some pepper. Cook the mixture, stirring often, until the onion is translucent — about 5 minutes. Pour in the stock, then add the potato slices. Reduce the heat, cover the pan, and simmer the liquid until a potato slice can be easily crushed with the back of a fork — 25 to 30 minutes.

While the stock is simmering, bring a large pan of water to the boil. Add the parsley leaves; as soon as the water returns to the boil, drain the leaves and refresh them under cold running water.

Purée the parsley and the stock-vegetable mixture together in a blender or food processor. Strain the purée through a sieve into a bowl and let it cool to room temperature. Cover the bowl with plastic film and refrigerate it until the soup is thoroughly chilled — at least 2 hours.

Purée the cubes of granita in a food processor just until the mixture is grainy. Transfer the cold parsley soup to six chilled soup bowls. Spoon some of the granita into each bowl; garnish with the mint sprigs and serve immediately.

Sweetcorn and Coriander Soup

Serves 4 as a first course
Working (and total) time: about 20 minutes

Calories **160**
Protein **5g**
Cholesterol **6mg**
Total fat **5g**
Saturated fat **2g**
Sodium **330mg**

10 g	unsalted butter	⅓ oz
1 tsp	safflower oil	1 tsp
1	onion, finely chopped	1
3	garlic cloves, finely chopped	3
1 tsp	ground cumin (optional)	1 tsp
1	sweet green pepper, seeded, deribbed and chopped	1
1	sweet red pepper, seeded, deribbed and chopped	1
1	green chili pepper (optional), seeded and finely chopped (caution, page 95)	1
1	ripe tomato, skinned, seeded, chopped	1
350 g	frozen sweetcorn kernels	12 oz
½ litre	unsalted chicken stock	16 fl oz
½ tsp	salt	½ tsp
2 tbsp	chopped fresh coriander	2 tbsp

Heat the butter and the oil together in a large, heavy-bottomed saucepan over medium heat. Add the onion, garlic and, if using, the cumin. Cook, stirring often, until the onion is translucent — about 5 minutes. Stir in all the peppers and cook them until they soften slightly — about 2 minutes more. Add the

tomato, sweetcorn, stock and salt. Reduce the heat and simmer the soup for 5 minutes. Stir in the coriander just before serving.

Cabbage and Caraway Soup

Serves 10 as a first course
Working time: about 45 minutes
Total time: about 1 hour and 45 minutes

Calories **75**
Protein **3g**
Cholesterol **1mg**
Total fat **4g**
Saturated fat **0g**
Sodium **165mg**

2 tbsp	safflower oil	2 tbsp
1.5 kg	cabbage, cored, quartered and thinly sliced	3 lb
1½ tsp	caraway seeds	1½ tsp
1 tsp	mustard seeds	1 tsp
½ tsp	salt	½ tsp
4 tbsp	red wine vinegar or white wine vinegar	4 tbsp
1 litre	unsalted chicken or veal stock	1¾ pints
4	garlic cloves, finely chopped	4
400 g	canned tomatoes, puréed with their juice	14 oz
¼ to ½ tsp	cayenne pepper	¼ to ½ tsp
2 tbsp	finely cut fresh dill, or 1 tbsp dried dill	2 tbsp

Heat the safflower oil in a large, heavy-bottomed saucepan over medium heat. Add the cabbage, caraway seeds, mustard seeds and salt. Cover the pan, and cook the cabbage, stirring occasionally, until it is wilted — about 25 minutes.

Add the vinegar and cook the mixture, stirring, for 1 minute. Pour in the stock and ¾ litre (1¼ pints) of cold water, then stir in the garlic, the tomato purée and the cayenne pepper. Reduce the heat and slowly bring the liquid to a simmer. Cook the soup gently for 45 minutes. Stir in the dill and serve immediately.

Hot and Sour Soup

Serves 8 as a first course
Working (and total) time: about 30 minutes

Calories **80**
Protein **5g**
Cholesterol **1mg**
Total fat **2g**
Saturated fat **0g**
Sodium **190mg**

1.5 litres	unsalted chicken stock	2½ pints
4 tbsp	rice vinegar	4 tbsp
2 tbsp	Chinese black vinegar or balsamic vinegar	2 tbsp
1 to 2 tsp	chili paste with garlic, or 5 to 10 drops Tabasco sauce	1 to 2 tsp
1 tbsp	low-sodium soy sauce or shoyu	1 tbsp
1 tbsp	dry sherry	1 tbsp
½ tsp	finely chopped garlic	½ tsp
1 to 2 tsp	finely chopped fresh ginger root	1 to 2 tsp
1	carrot, julienned	1
6	dried shiitake or Chinese black mushrooms, covered with boiling water and soaked for 20 minutes, stemmed, the caps thinly sliced	6
15 g	cloud-ear mushrooms (optional), covered with boiling water and soaked for 20 minutes, thinly sliced	½ oz
175 g	bamboo shoots (optional), rinsed and julienned	6 oz
2 tbsp	cornflour, mixed with 3 tbsp water	2 tbsp
250 g	firm tofu (bean curd), cut into thin strips	8 oz
3	spring onions, trimmed and sliced diagonally into ovals	3

Heat the stock in a large pan over medium-high heat. Add the rice vinegar, Chinese black vinegar, chili paste or Tabasco sauce, soy sauce, sherry, finely chopped garlic and ginger, julienned carrot and sliced shiitake or Chinese black mushrooms, and, if you are using them, the sliced cloud-ear mushrooms and bamboo shoots.

Bring the liquid to the boil, then stir in the cornflour mixture. Reduce the heat and simmer the soup, stirring, until it thickens slightly — 2 to 3 minutes. Gently stir in the tofu. Ladle the soup into bowls and garnish each serving with the spring onion slices.

Puréed Cauliflower Soup

Serves 8
Working time: about 45 minutes
Total time: about 1 hour

Calories **125**
Protein **7g**
Cholesterol **15mg**
Total fat **6g**
Saturated fat **3g**
Sodium **230mg**

15 g	unsalted butter	½ oz
3	onions (about 500 g/1 lb), thinly sliced	3
2 tsp	fresh thyme, or ½ tsp dried thyme	2 tsp
1 kg	cauliflower, cored, florets cut off	2 lb
7	garlic cloves, thinly sliced	7
1.5 litres	unsalted chicken stock	2½ pints
½ tsp	salt	½ tsp
½ tsp	grated nutmeg	½ tsp
	freshly ground black pepper	
100 g	low-fat ricotta cheese	3½ oz
2 tbsp	plain low-fat yogurt	2 tbsp
4 tbsp	single cream	4 tbsp
1 tsp	turmeric	1 tsp

Melt the butter in a large, heavy-bottomed saucepan over medium heat; then stir in the sliced onions and the thyme. Cover the pan and cook the onions, stirring frequently to keep them from browning, until they become very soft — about 15 minutes.

Reserve 125 g (4 oz) of the smallest cauliflower florets and set them aside for the garnish. Stir the remaining cauliflower florets and the garlic into the onion mixture. Cover the pan and cook the cauliflower for 15 minutes, stirring occasionally to prevent burning. Add the stock, salt, nutmeg and some pepper; simmer the mixture, covered, until the cauliflower is soft — about 20 minutes.

While the cauliflower is cooking, put the cheese and yogurt in a blender or food processor, and purée the mixture until it is very smooth. Transfer the mixture to a bowl, then whisk in the cream.

When the cauliflower is soft, purée the mixture in a blender or food processor in several batches. Return the batches of purée to the pan and keep it warm over low heat. Whisk in the cheese-yogurt mixture.

To prepare the garnish, combine the reserved cauliflower florets in a small pan with the turmeric and just enough water to cover the florets. Bring the water to the boil, reduce the heat, and simmer the florets until they are tender — about 7 minutes. Gently place several yellow florets on top of each portion of soup and serve at once.

Cauliflower Soup Provençale

Serves 6 as a first course
Working time: about 15 minutes
Total time: about 40 minutes

Calories **105**
Protein **5g**
Cholesterol **6mg**
Total fat **3g**
Saturated fat **1g**
Sodium **145mg**

750 g	cauliflower, cut into small florets, stems discarded	1½ lb
¾ litre	unsalted chicken stock	1¼ pints
2	ripe tomatoes, skinned, seeded and chopped	2
175 g	onion, chopped	6 oz
4	garlic cloves, finely chopped	4
1 tsp	dried basil	1 tsp
12.5 cl	dry white wine	4 fl oz
¼ tsp	salt	¼ tsp
	freshly ground black pepper	
2 tbsp	cut fresh dill or chopped fresh basil or flat-leaf parsley	2 tbsp
15 g	unsalted butter	½ oz

Blanch the cauliflower florets in 2 litres (3½ pints) of boiling water for 1 minute. Drain the florets in a colander and set them aside.

Pour the stock into a large pan. Add the tomatoes, onion, garlic, dried basil, wine, salt and some pepper, and bring the liquid to the boil. Reduce the heat and simmer the mixture for 10 minutes, stirring once.

Add the cauliflower and simmer the soup until the florets are tender — 10 to 15 minutes. Reduce the heat and let the soup simmer for 10 minutes to meld the flavours. Stir in the dill or other fresh herbs and the butter. Serve immediately.

Curried Yellow Split Pea Soup with Lamb and Mint

Serves 4
Working time: about 30 minutes
Total time: about 2 hours and 30 minutes

Calories **325**
Protein **20g**
Cholesterol **23mg**
Total fat **10g**
Saturated fat **1g**
Sodium **460mg**

175 g	dried yellow split peas, picked over and rinsed	6 oz
1 tbsp	safflower oil	1 tbsp
350 g	lamb shoulder, knuckle end, trimmed of fat	12 oz
1	onion, coarsely chopped	1
4 tbsp	thinly sliced celery	4 tbsp
2 tbsp	curry powder	2 tbsp
2	garlic cloves, finely chopped	2
1	small bay leaf	1
2 tbsp	chopped fresh mint	2 tbsp
1	carrot, thinly sliced	1
1 tsp	salt	1 tsp
¼ tsp	white pepper	¼ tsp
½	lemon, juice only	½
4	mint sprigs for garnish	4

In a large, heavy-bottomed saucepan, heat the safflower oil over medium-high heat and cook the lamb joint until it is brown on all sides — 3 to 5 minutes. Reduce the heat to medium and add the onion, celery and curry powder. Cook the vegetables, stirring constantly, until the onion turns translucent — 3 to 5 minutes. Add the garlic and continue to cook for 30 seconds, stirring to keep the mixture from burning. Add the peas, the bay leaf and 1.5 litres (2½ pints) of water. Bring the mixture to the boil, skim off any impurities, then add the chopped mint. Partially cover the pan, reduce the heat, and simmer the soup until the meat and the peas are tender — about 1 hour.

Remove the lamb joint, and when it is cool enough to handle, trim the meat from the bone; cut the meat into bite-size pieces and set them aside. Remove the bay leaf from the peas and discard it. Purée the peas in a blender or food processor, then return them to the pan. Add the lamb and carrot, and cook, covered, over medium heat until the carrot slices are tender — about 5 minutes. Season the soup with the salt, some pepper and the lemon juice. Serve in individual bowls, each garnished with a sprig of mint.

Caraway-Flavoured Celeriac Soup

Serves 6 as a first course
Working time: about 25 minutes
Total time: about 1 hour

Calories **145**
Protein **5g**
Cholesterol **7mg**
Total fat **7g**
Saturated fat **2g**
Sodium **315mg**

1 tbsp	safflower oil	1 tbsp
15 g	unsalted butter	½ oz
2	onions, chopped	2
750 g	celeriac, peeled and cut into 5 mm (¼ inch) cubes	1½ lb
1	carrot, coarsely chopped	1
2 litres	unsalted chicken stock	3½ pints
½ tsp	salt	½ tsp
	freshly ground black pepper	
½ tsp	caraway seeds	½ tsp
1 tbsp	fresh lemon juice	1 tbsp
2 tbsp	chopped fresh parsley	2 tbsp

Put 125 g (4 oz) of the cubed celeriac and ¼ litre (8 fl oz) of the stock into a small saucepan. Bring the mixture to the boil, reduce the heat, and simmer, covered, until the celeriac is tender — about 5 minutes. Set the saucepan aside.

Heat the oil and butter together in a large, heavy-bottomed saucepan over medium heat. Add the onions and cook them, stirring often, until they are translucent — about 10 minutes. Add the remaining celeriac, carrot and 1.5 litres (2½ pints) of the stock, and bring the liquid to the boil. Reduce the heat to medium, cover the pan and simmer the mixture for 15 minutes. Remove the lid and continue cooking the mixture until it is reduced by one third — about 10 minutes.

Remove the pan from the heat and purée the soup in batches in a blender, food processor or food mill. Return the soup to the pan and pour in the remaining stock along with the reserved celeriac cubes and their cooking liquid. Stir in the salt, pepper, caraway seeds, lemon juice and parsley. Briefly reheat and serve.

EDITOR'S NOTE: *This soup is also excellent served cold with cooked peeled shrimps floating on top.*

Batavian Endive Soup with Turnips and Apple

Serves 6 as a first course
Working time: about 20 minutes
Total time: about 50 minutes

Calories **105**
Protein **4g**
Cholesterol **3mg**
Total fat **4g**
Saturated fat **1g**
Sodium **135mg**

1 tbsp	virgin olive oil	1 tbsp
1	onion, chopped	1
2	medium turnips, chopped	2
1	carrot, chopped	1
1 tsp	fresh thyme, or ¼ tsp dried thyme	1 tsp
¼ tsp	salt	¼ tsp
	freshly ground black pepper	
12.5 cl	dry white wine	4 fl oz
1 tbsp	red wine vinegar	1 tbsp
¾ litre	unsalted chicken stock	1¼ pints
1	cooking apple, peeled, cored, chopped	1
350 g	Batavian endive, washed and shredded	12 oz
1	orange, grated rind only	1
4 tbsp	freshly grated Parmesan cheese	4 tbsp

Heat the oil in a large, heavy-bottomed saucepan over medium-high heat. Add the onion, turnips, carrot, thyme, salt and some pepper. Sauté the vegetables, stirring occasionally, until the onion is translucent — about 4 minutes. Pour in the wine and vinegar, and reduce the heat to medium. Cook the vegetables, covered, for 20 minutes.

Pour in the stock and ¾ litre (1¼ pints) of water, then add the chopped apple. Bring the liquid to the boil; then reduce the heat to maintain a simmer, cover the pan, and cook the soup for 5 minutes more. Add the Batavian endive and cook it until it is wilted — about 10 minutes. Sprinkle the orange rind on to the hot soup and serve it immediately with the cheese.

Peppery Peanut Soup

Serves 4
Working time: about 10 minutes
Total time: about 25 minutes

Calories **140**
Protein **6g**
Cholesterol **17mg**
Total fat **11g**
Saturated fat **4g**
Sodium **265mg**

10 g	unsalted butter	⅓ oz
60 g	celery, finely chopped	2 oz
1	garlic clove, finely chopped	1
1 tbsp	flour	1 tbsp
1 litre	unsalted chicken stock	1¾ pints
4 tbsp	single cream	4 tbsp
2 tbsp	peanut butter	2 tbsp
¼ tsp	salt	¼ tsp
⅛ to ¼ tsp	crushed hot red pepper flakes or cayenne pepper	⅛ to ¼ tsp
2	spring onions, trimmed and sliced diagonally into very thin ovals	2

Melt the butter in a large, heavy-bottomed saucepan over medium-low heat. Add the celery and garlic and cook them for 2 minutes. Stir in the flour and cook the mixture for 1 minute, stirring constantly. Whisk in the stock, peanut butter, salt and pepper, and simmer the mixture for 15 minutes. Stir in the spring onions and the cream, and let the soup heat through before serving.

White Bean Soup Cooked with a Bulb of Garlic

Serves 6
Working time: about 45 minutes
Total time: about 3 hours and 20 minutes
(includes soaking)

Calories **255**
Protein **15g**
Cholesterol **1mg**
Total fat **5g**
Saturated fat **1g**
Sodium **465mg**

360 g	dried haricot beans, picked over	12 oz
1.5 litres	unsalted chicken stock	2½ pints
1	onion	1
1	carrot, halved crosswise	1
1	stick celery, halved crosswise	1
1	leek, trimmed, split and washed thoroughly to remove all grit	1
1	bay leaf	1
2 tsp	fresh thyme, or ½ tsp dried thyme	2 tsp
1	large whole garlic bulb, papery outer skin removed	1
1 tsp	salt	1 tsp
1 tbsp	virgin olive oil	1 tbsp
3	ripe tomatoes, skinned, seeded and chopped	3
30 g	fresh parsley, preferably flat-leaf, chopped, plus 1 tbsp for garnish	3
	freshly ground black pepper	

Rinse the beans under cold running water, then put them into a large, heavy-bottomed saucepan, and pour in enough water to cover them by about 7.5 cm (3 inches). Discard any beans that float to the surface. Cover the pan, leaving the lid ajar, and slowly bring the liquid to the boil over medium-low heat. Boil the beans for 2 minutes, then turn off the heat and soak the beans, covered, for at least 1 hour. (Alternatively, soak the beans overnight in cold water.)

Drain the beans in a colander and return them to the pan. Pour in the stock, then add the onion, carrot, celery, leek, bay leaf and thyme. Slowly bring the liquid to the boil over medium-low heat. Reduce the heat to maintain a simmer, and cover the pan. Cook the beans, stirring occasionally and skimming any foam from the surface, until they are tender — 1 to 1½ hours. When the beans have been simmering for 30 minutes, add the whole garlic bulb and the salt.

Near the end of the cooking time, pour the olive oil into a heavy frying pan over high heat. Add the chopped tomatoes and cook them for 3 to 5 minutes, stirring frequently. Then stir in the 30 g (1 oz) of

chopped parsley and set the frying pan aside.

Drain the beans in a sieve set over a large bowl to catch the cooking liquid. Discard all the vegetables except the garlic. Return two thirds of the cooked beans to the saucepan. When the garlic bulb is cool enough to handle, separate it into its individual cloves and slip off their skins. Purée the garlic and the remaining beans in a food processor or food mill together with ¼ litre (8 fl oz) of the reserved cooking liquid. (Alternatively, press the garlic and beans through a sieve with a wooden spoon, then stir in ¼ litre/8 fl oz of the liquid.)

Transfer the garlic-bean purée to the pan with the beans and carefully stir in the remaining cooking liquid. Reheat the soup over low heat, then fold in the tomato mixture. Cook the soup for 1 to 2 minutes more. Season the soup with some pepper and serve it immediately, with the remaining tablespoon of parsley sprinkled over the top.

Chestnut Soup

Serves 4
Working time: about 20 minutes
Total time: about 1 hour and 10 minutes

Calories **380**
Protein **8g**
Cholesterol **6mg**
Total fat **9g**
Saturated fat **2g**
Sodium **220mg**

600 g	fresh chestnuts	1¼ lb
2 tsp	safflower oil	2 tsp
1	leek, trimmed, the green tops discarded, the stalks split, washed thoroughly, and cut into 1 cm (½ inch) pieces	1
12.5 cl	dry sherry	4 fl oz
125 g	mushrooms, stemmed, caps thinly sliced	4 oz
½ to ¾ litre	unsalted chicken stock	¾ to 1¼ pints
¼ tsp	salt	¼ tsp
¼ tsp	white pepper	¼ tsp
¼ litre	semi-skimmed milk	8 fl oz
1½ tbsp	sliced toasted almonds	1½ tbsp

Using a small, sharp knife, cut a shallow cross in the flat side of each chestnut. Drop the chestnuts into 1.5 litres (2½ pints) of boiling water and cook them for 10 minutes. Drain the chestnuts and let them cool slightly; peel them while they are still warm.

Heat the oil in a large, heavy-bottomed saucepan over medium heat. Add the leek pieces and sauté them, stirring frequently, until they are translucent — 4 to 5 minutes. Pour in the sherry, increase the heat to medium high, and cook the mixture until the liquid is reduced by three quarters — 3 to 4 minutes. Add the chestnuts, mushrooms and ½ litre (16 fl oz) of the stock. Bring the liquid to the boil, then reduce the heat and simmer the mixture, covered, until the chestnuts can be easily pierced with the tip of a sharp knife — 25 to 30 minutes.

Purée the mixture in a food processor, blender or food mill. Add the salt and pepper. Pour in the milk in stages, puréeing the mixture after each addition. (If you prefer a thinner soup, incorporate another ¼ litre/ 8 fl oz of stock into the purée.)

Return the puréed soup to the pan and reheat it for 2 to 3 minutes over medium heat. Garnish with the almonds before serving.

Gazpacho with Roasted Peppers

Serves 4 as a first course
Working time: about 50 minutes
Total time: about 1 hour and 50 minutes

Calories **70**
Protein **2g**
Cholesterol **0mg**
Total fat **4g**
Saturated fat **1g**
Sodium **170mg**

1	large sweet red pepper	1
1	large sweet green pepper	1
2	ripe tomatoes, skinned, seeded and coarsely chopped	2
2	sticks celery, thinly sliced	2
1	cucumber, peeled, halved lengthwise, seeded and cut into large chunks	1
2	garlic cloves, chopped	2
90 g	fresh watercress, coarsely chopped, plus 4 whole sprigs for garnish	3 oz
12.5 cl	unsalted veal or vegetable stock	4 fl oz
4 tbsp	fresh orange juice	4 tbsp
1 tbsp	fresh lemon juice	1 tbsp
1 tbsp	virgin olive oil	1 tbsp
¼ tsp	salt	¼ tsp
	freshly ground black pepper	

Preheat the grill. Grill the peppers 5 to 7.5 cm (2 to 3 inches) below the heat source, turning them often, until they are uniformly blistered and blackened — 12 to 15 minutes. Transfer the peppers to a bowl and tightly cover the bowl with plastic film. Let the peppers stand for 5 minutes — the trapped steam will loosen their skins.

Make a slit in one of the peppers and pour the juices that have collected inside it into the bowl. Peel the pepper from top to bottom. Halve the pepper lengthwise, then remove and discard the stem, seeds and ribs. Repeat the procedure with the other pepper.

Put the peppers and their juices into a food processor or blender along with the tomatoes, celery, cucumber, garlic, chopped watercress, stock, orange juice, lemon juice, oil, salt and some pepper. Process the mixture in short bursts until a coarse purée results. Transfer the gazpacho to a bowl; refrigerate it for at least 1 hour, then garnish it with the watercress sprigs and serve.

EDITOR'S NOTE: *This soup may be prepared as much as 24 hours in advance.*

Roquefort Onion Soup

Serves 8 as a first course
Working time: about 45 minutes
Total time: about 1 hour and 15 minutes

Calories **200**
Protein **7g**
Cholesterol **16mg**
Total fat **9g**
Saturated fat **4g**
Sodium **420mg**

15 g	unsalted butter	½ oz
1 tbsp	safflower oil	1 tbsp
1 kg	onions, thinly sliced	2 lb
2	garlic cloves, finely chopped	2
2 litres	unsalted chicken or veal stock	3½ pints
½ litre	dry white wine	16 fl oz
2 tsp	fresh thyme, or ½ tsp dried thyme	2 tsp
2 tsp	fresh lemon juice	2 tsp
½ tsp	salt	½ tsp
⅛ tsp	cayenne pepper	⅛ tsp
	freshly ground black pepper	
125 g	Roquefort cheese, crumbled	4 oz
1 tbsp	chopped fresh parsley	1 tbsp

Melt the butter and oil in a large, heavy-bottomed saucepan over medium-low heat. Add the onions and garlic and partially cover the pan. Cook for 3 minutes, stirring once. Remove the lid and continue cooking, stirring frequently, until the onions are browned — 20 to 35 minutes. Pour in 1.5 litres (2½ pints) of the stock and the wine, then add the thyme. Bring the liquid to the boil, lower the heat and simmer the mixture until it is reduced by one third — about 30 minutes. With a slotted spoon, remove about 150 g (5 oz) of the onions and set them aside.

Purée the soup in a blender, food processor or food mill. Return the soup to the pan and stir in the reserved onions. Pour in the remaining stock, then add the lemon juice, salt, cayenne pepper and some black pepper. Reheat the soup over medium heat for 2 minutes. In the meantime, combine the cheese and parsley in a small bowl and sprinkle the mixture over the soup just before serving.

one third and the carrots are soft — 8 to 10 minutes.

While the soup is boiling, bring the remaining stock to a simmer in a small saucepan over medium heat. Add the diced carrots and the sultanas and simmer them, covered, until the carrots are tender — about 5 minutes. Set the saucepan aside.

Purée the soup in batches in a blender, food processor or food mill. Return the soup to the pan over medium heat and add the diced carrots and sultanas with their cooking liquid. Stir in the cream, salt, some pepper, and the parsley. Simmer the soup until it is heated through — about 2 minutes — and serve at once.

Cream of Carrot Soup with Fresh Ginger

Serves 8 as a first course
Working time: about 30 minutes
Total time: about 1 hour

Calories **155**
Protein **4g**
Cholesterol **15mg**
Total fat **8g**
Saturated fat **3g**
Sodium **350mg**

1 kg	carrots	2 lb
2 tsp	safflower oil	2 tsp
10 g	unsalted butter	⅓ oz
275 g	onions, chopped	9 oz
4 tbsp	grated fresh ginger root	4 tbsp
2 litres	unsalted chicken stock	3½ pints
4 tbsp	sultanas, chopped	4 tbsp
12.5 cl	single cream	4 fl oz
¾ tsp	salt	¾ tsp
	freshly ground black pepper	
2 tbsp	chopped fresh parsley	2 tbsp

Cut two of the carrots into small dice and set them aside. Slice the remaining carrots into thin rounds.

Heat the oil and butter together in a large, heavy saucepan over medium heat. Add the onions and cook them, stirring occasionally, until they are golden — about 10 minutes. Add the carrot rounds and the ginger, and stir in 35 cl (12 fl oz) of the stock. Reduce the heat, cover the pan, and cook the mixture until the carrots are tender — about 20 minutes.

Pour 1.25 litres (2 pints) of the remaining stock into the pan and bring the liquid to the boil. Reduce the heat, cover the pan, and simmer the stock for 10 minutes. Remove the lid and increase the heat to high. Boil the soup, skimming the impurities from the surface several times, until the liquid is reduced by about

Chilled Curried Cucumber Soup

Serves 6 as a first course
Working time: about 20 minutes
Total time: about 1 hour and 20 minutes (includes chilling)

Calories **95**
Protein **5g**
Cholesterol **10mg**
Total fat **5g**
Saturated fat **3g**
Sodium **165mg**

30 g	fresh coriander, a few leaves reserved for garnish	1 oz
1	onion, quartered	1
2	cucumbers, peeled, quartered lengthwise, seeded and cut into chunks	2
12.5 cl	soured cream	4 fl oz
35 cl	plain low-fat yogurt	12 fl oz
1 tsp	curry powder	1 tsp
¼ tsp	salt	¼ tsp
¼ tsp	white pepper	¼ tsp
3 to 5	drops Tabasco sauce	3 to 5
30 cl	unsalted brown or chicken stock	½ pint

Chop the coriander in a food processor. Add the onion and cucumber chunks, and process them until they are finely chopped but not puréed. (Alternatively, you can chop the coriander by hand and grate or finely chop the onion and cucumbers.)

In a bowl, whisk the soured cream with ¼ litre (8 fl oz) of the yogurt, the curry powder, salt, white pepper and Tabasco sauce. Whisk in the cucumber mixture and the stock. Refrigerate the soup for at least 1 hour. Serve the soup in chilled bowls; garnish each portion with a dollop of the remaining yogurt and the reserved coriander leaves.

EDITOR'S NOTE: *This soup is even better when it is made a day in advance.*

Turnip Soup

Serves 4 as a first course
Working time: about 45 minutes
Total time: about 1 hour

Calories **130**
Protein **4g**
Cholesterol **13mg**
Total fat **6g**
Saturated fat **3g**
Sodium **250mg**

22 g	unsalted butter	¾ oz
500 g	small white turnips, peeled, quartered and thinly sliced crosswise	1 lb
¼ tsp	salt	¼ tsp
¼ tsp	grated nutmeg	¼ tsp
¾ litre	unsalted chicken stock	1¼ pints
3	small waxy potatoes	3
2 tbsp	loosely packed fresh chervil leaves or chopped fresh parsley	2 tbsp

Melt the butter in a large, heavy saucepan over medium heat. Stir in the turnips and cook them, stir-ring frequently, until they are golden-brown — approximately 20 minutes.

Season the turnips with the salt and nutmeg, and toss them gently. Remove and reserve 75 g (2½ oz) of the turnips to use as a garnish.

Pour the stock into the pan; then cover it and bring the liquid to the boil. Reduce the heat and simmer the soup for 20 minutes, skimming off any foam that rises to the surface.

At the end of the 20 minutes, peel and quarter the potatoes, then cut them crosswise into thin slices and add them to the soup. Simmer the soup until the potatoes are tender but still intact — 10 to 15 minutes. Taste the soup for seasoning and add more nutmeg if necessary. Garnish the soup with the chervil or parsley and the reserved turnips before serving.

Consommé

Serves 6 as a first course
Working time: about 30 minutes
Total time: about 1 hour

Calories **30**			
Protein **3g**	2 litres	unsalted brown, veal or chicken stock, thoroughly degreased (box, page 55)	3½ pints
Cholesterol **0mg**	3	egg whites	3
Total fat **0g**	125 g	lean beef, veal or chicken, trimmed of all fat and finely chopped	4 oz
Saturated fat **0g**	1	carrot, finely chopped	1
Sodium **270mg**	1	stick celery, finely chopped	1
	1	leek, trimmed, split and washed thoroughly, thinly sliced, or 1 onion, finely chopped	1
	1	sprig thyme, or ¼ tsp dried thyme	1
	1	bay leaf	1
	3	parsley sprigs, chopped	3
		freshly ground black pepper	
	½ tsp	salt	½ tsp

Pour the stock into a 4 litre (7 pint) pan and bring the liquid to the boil. While the stock is coming to the boil, put the egg whites into a bowl and beat them lightly. Stir the remaining ingredients into the egg whites.

Add the contents of the bowl to the boiling stock all at one time. Stir the mixture once or twice, and then stop stirring. Adjust the heat to maintain a slow simmer; do not allow the mixture to boil vigorously. The clarification ingredients should rise to the surface, forming a "raft", which will act as a filter. A hole or fissure should form in the raft; using a ladle or a spoon, gently enlarge the opening so that the stock can bubble up through it and over the filter. Simmer the consommé for 30 minutes.

Place a sieve or colander over a clean bowl and line it with several layers of muslin or a clean tea towel. When the consommé is done, ladle it from the hole in the raft, being careful not to break the raft, and strain it through the sieve into the bowl.

EDITOR'S NOTE: *Consommé is clarified stock. Although the egg whites are essential to the clarification process, they tend to draw out flavour. A variety of other ingredients — among them meat, aromatic vegetables, herbs and seasonings — are included for their flavour-giving properties.*

The consommé may be garnished with a variety of cut vegetables (overleaf). Typically, only one garnish is presented in each bowl; if the vegetables are cut into brunoise, however, they may be paired to provide intriguing contrasts of colour. Root vegetables such as carrots, turnips and swedes should be blanched in boiling water for 30 seconds before being used as garnishes.

A Simple Way to Clarify Stock

1 *ADDING THE CLARIFICATION MIXTURE. Bring 2 litres (3½ pints) of stock to the boil (for illustrative purposes, a clear fireproof casserole is used here). Pour in the freshly prepared clarification mixture (recipe above). Scrape the bowl, if necessary, to dislodge the last of the mixture.*

2 *STIRRING IN THE MIXTURE. With a long-handled wooden spoon, immediately stir the clarification mixture and the stock together to incorporate the former into the liquid. Adjust the heat so that the stock simmers; it should not be allowed to boil vigorously.*

3 *FORMING THE RAFT. Within a few minutes, the clarification mixture will float to the surface in a layer, creating a kind of raft. Locate a hole or fissure in the raft and gently enlarge it just enough to allow the stock to bubble through. Simmer the stock for 30 minutes more before straining it.*

Edible Adornments for Consommé

A Garnish of Tomato Julienne

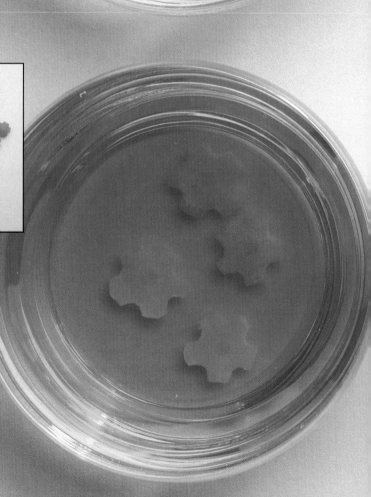

1 *REMOVING THE FLESH. Cut a shallow cross in the bottom of a tomato; blanch the tomato in boiling water for 15 seconds, then cool it immediately in cold water and peel off its skin. Place the tomato, stem end down, on a cutting board. Following the contour of the fruit, use a small knife to cut away the outer flesh in thin pieces (above).*

2 *CUTTING STRIPS. Lay a piece of tomato flat on the work surface and slice it lengthwise into strips about 3 mm (⅛ inch) wide (above). Repeat the process to julienne the other pieces; present the julienne in the soup as pictured on the right.*

Carrot Flowers

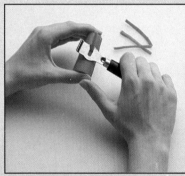

1 *SCORING THE CARROT. Cut a 5 cm (2 inch) segment from the stem end of a peeled carrot. Score a lengthwise groove in the segment by drawing a cannelle knife from one end to the other (above). Cut two or four additional evenly spaced channels in the segment. (Alternatively, notch an odd number of shallow grooves in the carrot segment with a paring knife.)*

2 *MAKING FLOWERS. Using a thin-bladed knife (here, a utility knife) shave thin rounds from the carrot segment to produce flowers. Blanch them for 30 seconds before adding them to consommé.*

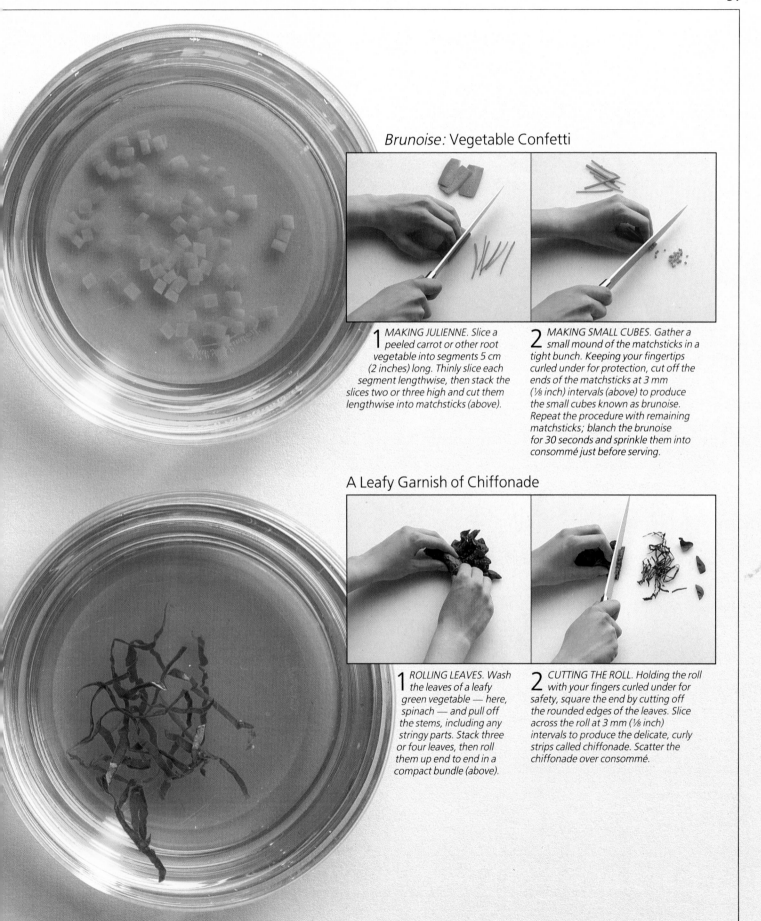

Brunoise: Vegetable Confetti

1 MAKING JULIENNE. Slice a peeled carrot or other root vegetable into segments 5 cm (2 inches) long. Thinly slice each segment lengthwise, then stack the slices two or three high and cut them lengthwise into matchsticks (above).

2 MAKING SMALL CUBES. Gather a small mound of the matchsticks in a tight bunch. Keeping your fingertips curled under for protection, cut off the ends of the matchsticks at 3 mm (⅛ inch) intervals (above) to produce the small cubes known as brunoise. Repeat the procedure with remaining matchsticks; blanch the brunoise for 30 seconds and sprinkle them into consommé just before serving.

A Leafy Garnish of Chiffonade

1 ROLLING LEAVES. Wash the leaves of a leafy green vegetable — here, spinach — and pull off the stems, including any stringy parts. Stack three or four leaves, then roll them up end to end in a compact bundle (above).

2 CUTTING THE ROLL. Holding the roll with your fingers curled under for safety, square the end by cutting off the rounded edges of the leaves. Slice across the roll at 3 mm (⅛ inch) intervals to produce the delicate, curly strips called chiffonade. Scatter the chiffonade over consommé.

Beef and Pasta Soup with Spring Onions and Red Pepper

Serves 4
Working time: about 30 minutes
Total time: about 1 hour and 30 minutes
(includes marinating)

Calories **230**
Protein **23g**
Cholesterol **40mg**
Total fat **7g**
Saturated fat **3g**
Sodium **445mg**

250 g	beef fillet, trimmed of all fat, cut into strips 2.5 cm (1 inch) long	8 oz
1 tbsp	low-sodium soy sauce or shoyu	1 tbsp
1 tbsp	dry sherry	1 tbsp
60 g	capelli d'angelo or other very thin pasta, broken into short lengths	2 oz
2 litres	unsalted brown stock	3½ pints
250 g	Chinese cabbage, cut into 5 mm (¼ inch) wide strips	8 oz
1	sweet red pepper, sliced into very thin strips	1
250 g	firm tofu (bean curd), cut into 1 cm (½ inch) cubes, each cube halved diagonally	8 oz
4	garlic cloves, finely chopped	4
1 tbsp	white vinegar	1 tbsp
3	spring onions, trimmed, green parts only, sliced diagonally into thin ovals	3
	freshly ground black pepper	

Combine the beef strips, soy sauce and sherry in a bowl. Marinate the beef at room temperature for at least 1 hour. Meanwhile, add the capelli d'angelo to 1 litre (1¾ pints) of boiling water with ½ teaspoon of salt. Start testing the pasta after 2 minutes and cook it until it is *al dente*. Drain the pasta, rinse it under cold running water to keep it from sticking together, and set it aside.

Bring the stock to the boil in a large pan. Add the Chinese cabbage and cook it for 5 minutes. Stir in the red pepper and cook the mixture until the cabbage and red pepper are tender — about 2 minutes more. Add the tofu, the capelli d'angelo, and the beef and its marinade. Reduce the heat and simmer the soup until the beef is cooked — about 2 minutes. Just before serving, stir in the garlic, vinegar, spring onions and a generous grinding of pepper.

Chicken Soup
with Carrots, Potatoes and Spinach

Serves 4
Working time: about 30 minutes
Total time: about 1 hour and 30 minutes

Calories **290**
Protein **27g**
Cholesterol **70mg**
Total fat **6g**
Saturated fat **2g**
Sodium **430mg**

1 kg	chicken, skinned, all visible fat removed	2 lb
1	onion, peeled and stuck with 2 cloves	1
1	stick celery	1
8 to 12	parsley stems	8 to 12
1	bay leaf	1
1 tsp	ground cumin	1 tsp
1	sprig fresh thyme, or ¼ tsp dried thyme	1
1	whole bulb of garlic, outer papery coating removed, bulb cut in half crosswise	1
½ tsp	salt	½ tsp
350 g	waxy potatoes, peeled and sliced	12 oz
500 g	carrots, sliced into 5mm (¼ inch) thick rounds	1 lb
125 g	fresh spinach, washed, stemmed and sliced into 1 cm (½ inch) wide strips	4 oz
	freshly ground black pepper	

Put the chicken into a large pan and add 1.5 litres (2½ pints) of water. Bring the water to the boil, then reduce the heat and simmer the chicken for 10 minutes, frequently skimming off the foam that rises to the surface. Add the onion, celery, parsley stems, bay leaf, cumin, thyme, garlic and salt, and continue simmering until the chicken is tender — about 45 minutes.

Place a colander over a large bowl and pour the contents of the pan into it. Stand the colander on a plate and leave the chicken to cool.

Return the broth to the pan and bring it to the boil. Add the potatoes, reduce the heat, and cover the pan; then simmer until the potatoes are just tender — about 10 minutes. Remove the potatoes with a slotted spoon and set them aside.

Add the carrots to the simmering broth, cover the pot, and continue to cook until the carrots are very tender — 15 to 20 minutes.

While the carrots are cooking, remove the meat from the chicken and either cut it or tear it with your fingers into bite-size pieces. Reserve the meat; discard the bones and the remaining solids in the colander.

When the carrots are cooked, purée half of them with half of the broth in a food processor or blender. Transfer the contents to a bowl; then purée the remaining carrots and broth. Pour all the liquid back into the pan. Add the potatoes, chicken and spinach leaves. Reheat the soup gently and season it with pepper.

Duck Soup with Chicory and Caramelized Pears

Serves 6
Working time: about 1 hour
Total time: about 3 hours

Calories **225**
Protein **20g**
Cholesterol **65mg**
Total fat **11g**
Saturated fat **5g**
Sodium **60mg**

2 kg	duck, skinned (opposite page), meat removed from bones and carcass, trimmed of all fat and cut into 1 cm (½ inch) cubes, the carcass, bones and giblets reserved	4 lb
1 tsp	Sichuan peppercorns, toasted and ground	1 tsp
1	onion, sliced	1
2	slices fresh ginger root, each about 3 mm (⅛ inch) thick	2
1	small head chicory, sliced	1
1 tbsp	safflower oil	1 tbsp
2	ripe but firm pears, peeled, quartered, cored and cut into thick slices	2
2 tsp	sugar	2 tsp
2 tbsp	red wine vinegar	2 tbsp
3	spring onions, trimmed, green parts sliced, white parts reserved for another use	3

Toss the cubes of duck meat with the ground peppercorns and refrigerate them while you make the stock.

To prepare the stock, first chop the duck carcass into three or four pieces with a large, heavy knife, a cleaver or poultry shears. Put the pieces into a large, heavy-bottomed saucepan or stockpot with the other bones and the giblets. Set the pan over medium heat and cook the bones and giblets for about 5 minutes. Pour in enough water (about 2 litres/3½ pints) to cover the bones, then add the onion and the ginger. Bring the water to the boil, skimming any foam from the surface. Simmer the stock for at least 2 hours. Strain it into a large bowl and degrease it (box, right).

While the stock is simmering, parboil the chicory. Bring 1 litre (1¾ pints) of water to the boil in a saucepan over medium-high heat. Add the chicory and cook it until it is tender — about 5 minutes. Drain the chicory and set it aside.

Heat the oil in another large, heavy-bottomed pan over medium heat. Add the cubes of duck meat and cook them, stirring frequently, until they are browned on all sides — about 5 minutes. Remove the cubes with a slotted spoon and set them aside.

Add the pear slices to the pan and cook them until they are translucent but still firm — about 5 minutes. Sprinkle the sugar over the pears and continue cooking them, stirring gently but constantly, until the sugar melts. Pour in the vinegar and cook the slices for 2 minutes more. Remove the pear slices and set them aside with the duck.

Pour the duck stock into the pan and bring the liquid to the boil, scraping the bottom and sides of the pan to dissolve the caramelized juices. Add the chicory slices, duck, caramelized pears and spring onions to the soup; return it to the boil and serve it at once.

Degreasing Soups and Stews

A pivotal step in making soups and stews as healthy as they can be is degreasing — the removal of fat from the surface of the cooking liquid. The means for achieving this are varied, both in the time they consume and in the tools they require.

The easiest and most effective degreasing method is to refrigerate the finished dish, then lift the congealed layer of fat from the surface. Because chilling takes time, it is ideal for soups, stews or stocks that are made ahead. To inhibit bacterial growth, a hot soup or stew should be quickly cooled to room temperature, then partially covered and refrigerated. The fat may then be removed before the dish is reheated. Stock, too, should be cooled rapidly: pour it into small containers and set them in a shallow bath of iced water. So that the stock will not sour, it should be covered and refrigerated only when it has cooled. Before transferring chilled stock to the freezer, scrape away all surface fat.

To degrease a hot dish just before serving it, use a soup ladle or a large, shallow spoon to skim off as much as you can; tip the pan, if need be, to pool the last bit of unwanted fat.

If you are making consommé, which must be served fat free, lightly draw an ice cube across the stock's surface; the fat will cling to the cube. Alternatively, blot up any remaining fat with paper towels: lay a corner or strip of towel directly on the fat, then immediately lift away the towel. Continue this process, always using a dry section of towel, to rid the surface of every drop of fat.

A hot liquid may also be defatted with a degreasing cup, a curious-looking clear pitcher whose spout rises from the bottom rather than the top. First strain the soup, stew or stock, then ladle the strained liquid into the degreasing cup and let it stand; the fat will rise to the surface. Tipping the cup at a slight angle, slowly pour the liquid from the spout; stop pouring when the layer of fat nears the spout opening at the bottom. Rinse the cup with hot water, then repeat the procedure to degrease the remaining liquid.

Skinning a Duck

1 *REMOVING THE WINGS. Pull out and discard the pockets of fat just inside the duck's tail cavity. Cut off and discard the tail and the flap of neck skin. With the duck breast side down, pull a wing away from the body and cut through the joint with a boning knife (below). Sever the other wing likewise; use the wings for stock.*

2 *SPLITTING THE SKIN. Cut through the skin along the backbone from one end of the bird to the other as demonstrated below. Turn the duck on to its back and make another straight cut from end to end to split the skin on the breast side.*

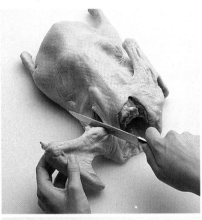
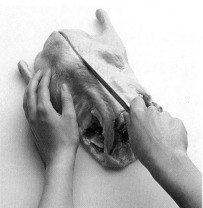

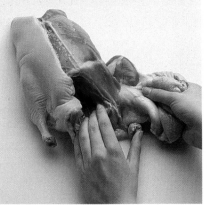

3 *SKINNING THE BODY. At one end of the cut on the breast side, pull away a small flap of skin; insert the knife tip between skin and flesh. Holding the skin taut, cut against it with short strokes to detach the skin, lifting it off with your free hand (above). Turn the bird on to its breast; starting at the neck end of the split, detach the skin on the same half of the duck from the neck to below the thigh joint.*

4 *SKINNING THE LEG. Turn the duck on to its back again and gather the detached skin in one hand. Steadying the bird with your other hand, pull the skin down over the leg as shown. (Where the skin adheres firmly to the meat, pull it taut and cut it away.) Trim off any skin still attached to the tail area. Repeat Steps 3 and 4 to skin the duck's other side.*

Pour the stock into a large pan. Add the remaining sage, the carrots, the remaining salt and some pepper. Bring the liquid to a simmer over medium heat and cook it for about 10 minutes.

While the stock is simmering, pour the oil into a non stick or heavy frying pan over medium-high heat. Arrange the meatballs in the hot oil, taking care that they do not touch one another. Cook the meatballs on one side until they are well browned — 3 to 5 minutes. Continue to cook the meatballs, turning them frequently, until they are browned on all sides — about 5 to 7 minutes more.

With a slotted spoon, transfer the meatballs to the simmering stock mixture in the pan. Add the pasta and cook it until it is *al dente* — about 4 minutes.

Transfer the soup to individual serving bowls; garnish with the sage leaves if you are using them, and serve immediately.

Veal and Noodle Soup with Sage

Serves 6
Working time: about 40 minutes
Total time: about 1 hour and 10 minutes

Calories **240**
Protein **17g**
Cholesterol **75mg**
Total fat **7g**
Saturated fat **2g**
Sodium **385mg**

350 g	lean veal, finely chopped or minced	12 oz
1	egg, beaten with 1 egg white	1
1½ tbsp	chopped fresh sage, or 2 tsp dried sage	1½ tbsp
2 tbsp	freshly grated Parmesan or pecorino cheese	2 tbsp
2	slices day-old white bread, crumbled	2
1	ripe tomato, seeded and finely chopped	1
200 g	very finely chopped onion	7 oz
5	garlic cloves, finely chopped	5
½ tsp	salt	½ tsp
	freshly ground black pepper	
1 litre	unsalted veal stock	1¾ pints
2	carrots, thinly sliced	2
1 tbsp	safflower oil	1 tbsp
125 g	capelli d'angelo (angel's hair pasta)	4 oz
	fresh sage leaves for garnish (optional)	

In a large bowl, combine the veal, egg mixture, 1 tablespoon of the sage, the cheese, bread, tomato, onion, garlic, ¼ teaspoon of the salt and some pepper. Cover the bowl with plastic film and refrigerate it for 30 minutes. Form the chilled mixture into 18 meatballs, each about 2.5 cm (1 inch) in diameter. Set the meatballs aside.

Sake-Simmered Velvet Chicken Soup

THE "VELVET" IN THE TITLE REFERS TO THE SMOOTH COATING OF CORNFLOUR THAT ENVELOPS THE CHICKEN, SEALING IN ITS SUCCULENT JUICES.

Serves 2
Working time: about 30 minutes
Total time: about 45 minutes

Calories **340**
Protein **30g**
Cholesterol **70mg**
Total fat **6g**
Saturated fat **2g**
Sodium **320mg**

250 g	boneless chicken breast or thigh meat, skinned, trimmed of all fat and cut into 1 cm (½ inch) cubes	8 oz
1 tbsp	cornflour	1 tbsp
60 cl	unsalted chicken stock	1 pint
4 tbsp	sake or rice wine	4 tbsp
1 tsp	low-sodium soy sauce or shoyu	1 tsp
1 to 2 tbsp	finely chopped fresh ginger root	1 to 2 tbsp
2	carrots, sliced into 1 cm (½ inch) thick rounds	2
2 or 3	parsnips, peeled, sliced into 1 cm (½ inch) thick rounds	2 or 3
4	spring onions, trimmed, sliced diagonally into thin ovals	4

Pour 1 litre (1¾ pints) of water into a saucepan and bring it to the boil. Toss the chicken cubes with the cornflour to coat them evenly, then add them to the boiling water; stir with a slotted spoon to separate the cubes. When the water returns to the boil, remove the chicken pieces and set them aside. Discard the water.

Add the stock to the saucepan along with the sake or rice wine, the soy sauce and the ginger. Bring the liquid to the boil, then add the chicken cubes, carrots and parsnips. Reduce the heat to low, cover the pan, and simmer the soup for 15 minutes. Stir the spring onions into the soup 2 minutes before serving.

Lamb and Wild Rice Soup

Serves 6
Working time: about 50 minutes
Total time: about 2 hours

Calories **375**
Protein **19g**
Cholesterol **1mg**
Total fat **13g**
Saturated fat **6g**
Sodium **275mg**

1 tbsp	safflower oil	1 tbsp
2	lamb shoulder joints, knuckle end (about 1kg/2 lb), trimmed of fat	2
750 g	onions, coarsely chopped	1½ lb
½ litre	dry white wine	16 fl oz
400 g	canned tomatoes, drained and chopped	14 oz
¾ litre	unsalted chicken or veal stock	1¼ pints
1	carrot, sliced into 5 mm (¼ inch) thick rounds	1
8	garlic cloves, chopped	8
1	stick celery, chopped	1
	freshly ground black pepper	
½ tsp	salt	½ tsp
1½ tbsp	fresh rosemary, or 1 tsp dried rosemary	1½ tbsp
160 g	wild rice	5½ oz

Heat the oil in a large, heavy frying pan over medium-high heat. Sauté the lamb joints in the pan until they are dark brown all over — about 15 minutes. Transfer the browned lamb joints to a stockpot or large, heavy-bottomed saucepan.

Reduce the heat under the frying pan to medium. Add the onions and cook them, stirring frequently, until they are lightly browned — 10 to 15 minutes.

Add the onions to the pot. Return the pan to the heat and immediately pour in the wine. With a wooden spoon, scrape up the caramelized pan juices from the bottom, stirring well to dissolve them. Add the tomatoes and boil the mixture until it is reduced by half — about 5 minutes. Pour the reduced liquid into the pot, then add the stock, 2.5 litres (4 pints) of water, the carrot, garlic, celery and some pepper.

Place the pot over medium heat and bring the mixture to a strong simmer, skimming off any foam that rises to the surface. Stir in the salt and rosemary. Reduce the heat and gently simmer the soup until the lamb is tender — 1½ to 2 hours.

After the meat has cooked for 1 hour, put the rice into a saucepan with ¼ litre (8 fl oz) of water and bring the liquid to a simmer over medium heat. Reduce the heat to low and cook the rice slowly until all of the water is absorbed — about 15 minutes. Set the rice aside.

Transfer the lamb joints to a clean work surface. When they are cool enough to handle, remove the meat from the bones. Cut the meat into small pieces; discard the bones. Return the meat to the pot. Add the partially cooked rice and simmer the soup until the rice is tender — about 20 minutes. Serve the soup hot.

Chicken, Aubergine and Tomato Soup

Serves 4
Working (and total) time: about 1 hour

Calories **280**
Protein **27g**
Cholesterol **65mg**
Total fat **9g**
Saturated fat **4g**
Sodium **380mg**

2 litres	unsalted chicken stock	3½ pints
4	garlic cloves, finely chopped	4
1	lemon, juice only	1
	freshly ground black pepper	
4	chicken breasts, skinned and boned (about 500 g/1 lb)	4
1 tbsp	chopped fresh mint	1 tbsp
1.25 kg	ripe tomatoes, skinned, seeded and coarsely chopped, or 800 g (28 oz) canned tomatoes, drained and chopped	2½ lb
1 tbsp	fresh thyme, or ¾ tsp dried thyme	1 tbsp
350 g	unpeeled aubergine, cut into 1 cm (½ inch) cubes	12 oz
60 g	feta cheese, soaked 10 minutes in cold water to remove some of its salt, drained and crumbled	2 oz

Bring the stock to the boil in a large, heavy-bottomed saucepan. Add the garlic, half of the lemon juice and a generous grinding of pepper; reduce the heat and add the chicken. Poach the chicken at a simmer until the meat feels springy to the touch — about 5 minutes.

Use a slotted spoon to remove the chicken from the poaching liquid. When the chicken is cool enough to handle, cut it into small cubes and put the cubes in a bowl. Toss the chicken with the mint and the remaining lemon juice, and set it aside to marinate.

Add the tomatoes and thyme to the stock, and simmer the liquid for 10 minutes. Add the aubergine and cook for 5 minutes more. Stir in the chicken and its marinade and simmer the soup for 2 minutes. Serve the soup with the cheese sprinkled on top.

Chicken Soup with Chilies, Cabbage and Rice

Serves 4
Working time: about 20 minutes
Total time: about 1 hour

Calories **285**
Protein **20g**
Cholesterol **60mg**
Total fat **11g**
Saturated fat **2g**
Sodium **275mg**

1 tbsp	safflower oil	1 tbsp
750 g	chicken thighs, skinned, fat trimmed	1½ lb
1	garlic clove, finely chopped	1
3	spring onions, trimmed and sliced into thin rounds	3
½ litre	unsalted chicken stock	16 fl oz
1 tbsp	fresh thyme, or ¾ tsp dried thyme	1 tbsp
	freshly ground black pepper	
¼ tsp	salt	¼ tsp
90 g	long-grain rice	3 oz
2	large dried mild chili peppers, stemmed, split lengthwise and seeded	2
1	large carrot, julienned	1
175 g	shredded Chinese cabbage	6 oz

Heat the safflower oil in a large, heavy-bottomed saucepan over medium-high heat. Add the chicken thighs and sauté them, turning them frequently, until they are evenly browned — 3 to 4 minutes. Push the chicken to one side of the pan; add the garlic and spring onions and cook them for 1 minute, stirring constantly. Pour in the stock and ¾ litre (1¼ pints) of water. Add the thyme and some pepper, and bring the liquid to the boil. Reduce the heat to maintain a simmer and cook the mixture, partially covered, for 20 minutes. Skim any impurities from the surface and simmer the liquid for 20 minutes more.

While the stock is simmering, bring ¼ litre (8 fl oz) of water and ⅛ teaspoon of the salt to the boil in another saucepan. Add the rice and stir once, then reduce the heat and cover the pan. Simmer the rice until all of the water is absorbed — about 20 minutes.

While the rice is cooking, pour ¼ litre (8 fl oz) of boiling water over the chilies and soak for 15 minutes. Purée the chilies with their soaking liquid in a blender. (Or pulverize the soaked chilies with a mortar and pestle, gradually adding the liquid to incorporate it into the paste.)

With a slotted spoon, remove the chicken thighs from the pan and set them aside. When the chicken is cool enough to handle, remove the meat from the bones with your fingers and cut it into small pieces; discard the bones. Return the chicken pieces to the pan. Add the carrot, cabbage, rice and the remaining salt. Increase the heat to maintain a simmer and cook the soup until the carrot is tender — 3 to 4 minutes. Strain the chili purée through a fine sieve into the soup. Stir to incorporate the purée and serve the soup at once.

Beef Soup with Brussels Sprouts and Sweet Potato

Serves 4
Working time: about 30 minutes
Total time: about 1 hour and 30 minutes

Calories **225**
Protein **28g**
Cholesterol **75mg**
Total fat **7g**
Saturated fat **3g**
Sodium **190mg**

500 g	beef shin bones	1 lb
500 g	lean beef, finely diced	1 lb
1	small onion, thinly sliced	1
1	garlic clove, finely chopped	1
1	small bay leaf	1
125 g	Brussels sprouts, trimmed and halved lengthwise	4 oz
150 g	sweet potato, peeled and cut into 2 cm (¾ inch) cubes	5 oz
1 tsp	finely chopped fresh rosemary, or ½ tsp dried rosemary	1 tsp
¼ tsp	salt	¼ tsp
	freshly ground black pepper	

Place the shin bones, beef, onion, garlic and bay leaf in a large, heavy-bottomed saucepan. Pour in 2.5 litres (4 pints) of water and bring it to the boil. Reduce the heat to maintain a strong simmer. Cook the mixture, partially covered, for 1 hour, occasionally skimming off the impurities that rise to the surface.

Remove and discard the bones and bay leaf. Increase the heat to high and cook the mixture until the liquid is reduced to about ¾ litre (1¼ pints) — 10 to 15 minutes. Add the Brussels sprouts, sweet potato and rosemary. Reduce the heat and simmer the soup until the vegetables are tender — 8 to 10 minutes. Stir in the salt and some pepper, and serve the soup immediately.

Pork Soup with Chinese Cabbage

Serves 6
Working (and total) time: about 25 minutes

Calories **230**
Protein **20g**
Cholesterol **50mg**
Total fat **5g**
Saturated fat **1g**
Sodium **300mg**

4 tbsp	rice wine or dry sherry	4 tbsp
2 tbsp	cornflour	2 tbsp
1 tbsp	finely chopped fresh ginger root	1 tbsp
500 g	pork fillet, trimmed of all fat, thinly sliced across the grain	1 lb
125 g	vermicelli or thin egg noodles	4 oz
¼ tsp	salt	¼ tsp
6	dried Asian mushrooms, covered with boiling water and soaked for 20 minutes, stemmed and thinly sliced, soaking liquid reserved	6
1.5 litres	unsalted chicken stock	2½ pints
3 tbsp	rice vinegar	3 tbsp
2 tsp	soya bean paste	2 tsp
250 g	Chinese cabbage, thinly sliced	8 oz
6 tbsp	fresh coriander leaves	6 tbsp
½ tsp	dark sesame oil	½ tsp

Pour the wine into a non-reactive bowl and stir in the cornflour and ginger. Add the pork and stir gently to coat it with the liquid. Set the bowl aside.

Add the vermicelli or noodles to 1 litre (1¾ pints) of boiling water with ¼ teaspoon of salt. Start testing the pasta after 3 minutes and cook it until it is *al dente*. Drain and rinse it under cold water and set it aside.

Carefully pour 12.5 cl (4 fl oz) of the mushroom-soaking liquid into a measuring jug, leaving the grit behind, then pour the measured liquid into a large, heavy-bottomed pan. Add the mushrooms, stock, vinegar and bean paste. Bring the liquid to the boil, then stir in the pork slices with their marinade and the cabbage. Return the liquid to the boil and add the vermicelli, coriander and sesame oil. Cook the soup until the pasta is heated through — about 2 minutes. Transfer the soup to a warmed bowl and serve it at once.

Turkey-Lentil Soup

Serves 6
Working time: about 15 minutes
Total time: about 1 hour

Calories **220**			
Protein **22g**	750 g	turkey drumsticks, skinned	1 ½ lb
Cholesterol **45mg**		freshly ground black pepper	
Total fat **5g**	2 tsp	safflower oil	2 tsp
Saturated fat **1g**	1	small onion, thinly sliced	1
Sodium **185mg**	190 g	lentils, picked over and rinsed	7 oz
	1	small bay leaf	1
	1	small carrot, thinly sliced	1
	1	small courgette, thinly sliced	1
	1	stick celery, thinly sliced	1
	1	ripe tomato, skinned, seeded and coarsely chopped	1
	½ tsp	finely chopped fresh sage, or ¼ tsp dried sage	½ tsp
	⅜ tsp	salt	⅜ tsp

Sprinkle the drumsticks with some pepper. Heat the oil in a large, heavy-bottomed saucepan over medium heat. Add the drumsticks and cook them, turning them frequently, until they are evenly browned — 2 to 3 minutes. Push the drumsticks to one side of the pan, then add the onion and cook it until it is translucent — 2 to 3 minutes.

Pour 1.25 litres (2 pints) of water into the pan. Add the lentils and bay leaf, and bring the water to the boil. Reduce the heat to maintain a simmer and cook the lentils, covered, for 20 minutes. Skim off any impurities that have risen to the surface. Continue cooking the mixture until the juices run clear from a drumstick pierced with the tip of a sharp knife — about 20 minutes more.

Remove the drumsticks and set them aside. When they are cool enough to handle, slice the meat from the bones and cut it into small pieces; discard the bones. Remove and discard the bay leaf. Add the carrot, courgette, celery and tomato to the soup and simmer until the vegetables are tender — about 5 minutes. Add the turkey meat, sage and salt, and continue cooking the soup until the vegetables are tender — about 2 minutes more. Serve hot.

Lamb Broth
with Winter Vegetables

Serves 6
Working time: about 15 minutes
Total time: about 2 hours

Calories **205**
Protein **9g**
Cholesterol **35mg**
Total fat **14g**
Saturated fat **7g**
Sodium **225mg**

1 tbsp	safflower oil	1 tbsp
1	small onion, thinly sliced, slices separated into rings	1
750 g	lamb shoulder, knuckle end, trimmed	1½ lb
4 tbsp	pearl barley	4 tbsp
1	bay leaf	1
1 tsp	chopped fresh thyme, or ¼ tsp dried thyme	1 tsp
1	garlic clove, finely chopped	1
½ tsp	salt	½ tsp
¼ tsp	crushed black peppercorns	¼ tsp
1	turnip, peeled and cut into 1 cm (½ inch) cubes	1
1	small swede, peeled and cut into 1 cm (½ inch) cubes	1
1	carrot, cut into 1 cm (½ inch) cubes	1

Heat the oil in a large, heavy-bottomed saucepan over medium heat. Add the onion rings and cook them until they are browned — about 8 minutes. Add the lamb, barley, bay leaf, thyme, garlic, salt and crushed peppercorns. Pour in 3 litres (5¼ pints) of water and bring the liquid to the boil. Reduce the heat and simmer the mixture, partially covered, for 1¼ hours.

Remove the bay leaf and discard it. Remove the lamb joint from the pan; when the lamb is cool enough to handle, slice the meat from the bone and cut it into small cubes. Return the lamb cubes to the pan. Simmer the soup, uncovered, over medium heat until it is reduced by half — about 15 minutes. Add the turnip, swede and carrot, cover the pan, and simmer the soup until the vegetables are tender — about 15 minutes more. Serve immediately.

Vegetable Soup with Grilled Chicken

Serves 4
Working time: about 30 minutes
Total time: about 1 hour

Calories **255**
Protein **16g**
Cholesterol **25mg**
Total fat **10g**
Saturated fat **2g**
Sodium **320mg**

2	chicken breasts, skinned and boned (about 250 g/8 oz)	2
1 tsp	olive oil	1 tsp
1	lime, juice only	1
	freshly ground black pepper	
1	large red onion, chopped	1
2	garlic cloves, finely chopped	2
1.5 litres	unsalted chicken stock	2½ pints
500 g	ripe plum tomatoes, skinned, seeded and chopped, or 400 g (14 oz) canned tomatoes, drained and chopped	1 lb
⅛ tsp	ground coriander	⅛ tsp

⅛ tsp	cayenne pepper	⅛ tsp
¼ tsp	ground cumin	¼ tsp
½ tsp	dried oregano	½ tsp
1	carrot, julienned	1
1	courgette, julienned	1
125 g	water chestnuts, julienned	4 oz
1 tbsp	finely cut chives	1 tbsp
Tortilla-strip garnish		
3	corn tortillas	3
1 tbsp	olive oil	1 tbsp

Using a boning knife or other thin-bladed knife, cut each chicken breast horizontally into two thin, flat pieces. Set the pieces on a large plate, dribble the teaspoon of oil and the lime juice over them and sprinkle them with some pepper. Let the chicken marinate while you make the rest of the soup.

Combine the onion, garlic and stock in a saucepan over medium-high heat. Bring the stock to the boil, then add the tomatoes, coriander, cayenne pepper, cumin, oregano and salt. Reduce the heat and simmer the mixture for 20 minutes. Add the carrot, courgette and water chestnuts, and simmer them until they are tender — about 6 minutes.

Just before the vegetables are done, prepare the chicken and the garnish. Preheat the grill. Remove the chicken from the marinade and cook it until it is firm to the touch — about 2 minutes on each side. Cut the pieces on the diagonal into thin slices.

Brush the tortillas with the tablespoon of olive oil and cut them into thin strips. Spread the strips out on a baking sheet and grill them until they are crisp and lightly browned — about 3 minutes.

Arrange the chicken slices on top of the soup and sprinkle it with the chives. Serve the tortilla strips in a bowl separately.

Turkey Goulash Soup

Serves 6
Working time: about 30 minutes
Total time: about 45 minutes

Calories **260**
Protein **24g**
Cholesterol **40mg**
Total fat **6g**
Saturated fat **1g**
Sodium **290mg**

2 tsp	safflower oil	2 tsp
500 g	onions, thinly sliced	1 lb
2	sweet green peppers, seeded, deribbed and cut into 2 cm (¾ inch) squares	2
2 tbsp	paprika, preferably Hungarian	2 tbsp
¼ tsp	ground cumin	¼ tsp
	freshly ground black pepper	
2 litres	unsalted chicken stock	3½ pints
2 tbsp	cornflour	2 tbsp
125 g	wide egg noodles	4 oz
500 g	turkey escalopes, sliced across the grain into 5 cm (2 inch) long strips	1 lb
⅜ tsp	salt	⅜ tsp

Heat the safflower oil in a large, heavy-bottomed saucepan over medium heat. Add the sliced onions and cook them until they are browned — about 15 minutes. Stir in the green peppers, paprika, cumin, some black pepper and all except 4 tablespoons of the stock. Combine the cornflour and the reserved stock, and add this mixture to the pan. Simmer the stock, partially covered, for 20 minutes.

While the stock is simmering, add the noodles to 2 litres (3½ pints) of boiling water with ½ teaspoon of salt. Start testing the noodles after 5 minutes and cook them until they are *al dente*. Drain the noodles, rinse them under cold running water, and set them aside.

Add the turkey strips to the simmering stock and poach them until they are opaque — 3 to 4 minutes. Stir in the noodles and the ⅜ teaspoon of salt. Cook the soup for 2 minutes more; serve at once.

Turkey Soup with Lemon-Celery Dumplings

Serves 6
Working time: about 45 minutes
Total time: about 2 hours and 20 minutes

Calories **320**
Protein **33g**
Cholesterol **70mg**
Total fat **8g**
Saturated fat **3g**
Sodium **515mg**

1 kg	turkey wings, without tips	2 lb
2	carrots, sliced into thin rounds	2
2	onions, coarsely chopped	2
¾ tsp	ground allspice	¾ tsp
2	sticks celery, thinly sliced	2
2 tbsp	fresh lemon juice	2 tbsp
5	garlic cloves, finely chopped	5
½ tsp	salt	½ tsp
	freshly ground black pepper	

Lemon-celery dumplings		
190 g	plain flour	6½ oz
2 tsp	baking powder	2 tsp
¼ tsp	salt	¼ tsp
⅛ tsp	cayenne pepper	⅛ tsp
3 tbsp	finely chopped celery leaves	3 tbsp
1 tbsp	safflower oil	1 tbsp
15 g	unsalted butter, melted	½ oz
12.5 cl	semi-skimmed milk	4 fl oz
1 tbsp	fresh lemon juice	1 tbsp
1 tsp	grated lemon rind	1 tsp

Place the turkey wings in a large, heavy-bottomed pan. Pour in 3 litres (5¼ pints) of water and bring it to the boil. Reduce the heat to medium and cook the turkey for 5 minutes, skimming off any impurities that collect on the surface of the liquid. Pour in 12.5 cl (4 fl oz) of cold water, and simmer the turkey for 20 minutes,

skimming as necessary. Add the carrots, onions, allspice, celery, lemon juice, garlic, salt and some pepper. Simmer the mixture until the turkey is quite tender — about 1½ hours.

About half an hour before the turkey is done, prepare the dumpling dough: sift the flour, baking powder, salt and cayenne pepper into a large bowl. Stir in the celery leaves, oil and butter to obtain a dry paste. Whisk in the milk 4 tablespoons at a time, then whisk in the lemon juice and lemon rind until the dough becomes smooth and elastic. Cover the bowl with plastic film and refrigerate it.

When the turkey is tender, strain the liquid into a large bowl. Remove the wings from the strainer and set them aside. Degrease the liquid (box, page 55). Purée the vegetables with a little of the cooking liquid in a blender or food processor. Return the purée and the degreased liquid to the pan.

When the turkey wings are cool enough to handle, peel off and discard their skin. Remove the meat from the bones; discard the bones. Cut the meat into 1 cm (½ inch) pieces and return it to the soup.

Bring the soup to a simmer. Spoon heaped teaspoons of the dough directly into the soup, rinsing the spoon in cold water after each dumpling floats free. Simmer the dumplings on the first side for 5 minutes, then gently turn them over and simmer them on the second side until they are lightly puffed up — 3 to 5 minutes more. Serve the soup and dumplings immediately.

EDITOR'S NOTE: *If the upper parts of turkey wings — which contain most of the meat — are not available, drumsticks may be substituted.*

Beef and Wild Mushroom Soup

Serves 8
Working time: about 50 minutes
Total time: about 1 hour

Calories **185**
Protein **17g**
Cholesterol **40mg**
Total fat **8g**
Saturated fat **2g**
Sodium **375mg**

10	dried shiitake or Asian black mushrooms, covered with ½ litre (16 fl oz) of boiling water and soaked for 20 minutes	10
1.5 litres	unsalted chicken stock	2½ pints
2 tbsp	safflower oil	2 tbsp
500 g	rump steak, trimmed of fat and cut into 1 cm (½ inch) wide strips	1 lb
5	garlic cloves, finely chopped	5
2	onions, finely chopped	2
125 g	fresh shiitake or field mushrooms, stems trimmed, thinly sliced	4 oz
250 g	button mushrooms, stems trimmed, thinly sliced	8 oz
½ tsp	salt	½ tsp
12.5 cl	Madeira, dry sherry or Marsala	4 fl oz
	freshly ground black pepper	
2 tbsp	low-sodium soy sauce or shoyu	2 tbsp
2 tbsp	chopped fresh parsley, preferably flat-leaf	2 tbsp

Remove the soaked mushrooms from their liquid; reserve the liquid. Cut off and discard the stems. Thinly slice the caps and set them aside. Slowly pour all but about 12.5 cl (4 fl oz) of the mushroom-soaking liquid into a large pan, leaving the grit behind; discard the gritty liquid. Add the chicken stock to the pan and bring the liquid to a simmer.

While the liquid is heating, pour 1 tablespoon of the oil into a large, heavy frying pan over medium-high heat. When the oil is hot, add the beef and sauté it, stirring constantly, for 2 minutes. Remove the beef and set it aside.

Pour the remaining oil into the frying pan. Add the chopped garlic and onion and sauté them for 30 seconds, stirring constantly. Stir in all of the soaked and fresh mushrooms and ¼ teaspoon of the salt. Sauté the mixture, stirring frequently, for 5 minutes. Pour in the Madeira, sherry or Marsala and stir to scrape up and dissolve any caramelized bits. Add the contents of the frying pan to the stock with the remaining salt, some pepper and the soy sauce. Simmer for 20 minutes.

Stir in the sautéed beef strips and cook for 1 minute more. Serve garnished with the chopped parsley.

Cream of Chicken Soup

Serves 6
Working time: about 20 minutes
Total time: about 2 hours

Calories **240**			
Protein **34g**	1.5 kg	chicken	3 lb
Cholesterol **105mg**	1.5 litres	unsalted vegetable stock	2½ pints
Total fat **10g**	1	bay leaf	1
Saturated fat **5g**	2	blades of mace	2
Sodium **160mg**	1	small bunch of parsley	1
	½ tsp	salt	½ tsp
	15 g	unsalted butter, softened	½ oz
	15 g	flour	½ oz
	3 tbsp	double cream	3 tbsp
		freshly ground black pepper	
		chopped parsley for garnish	

Wipe the chicken well with paper towels and place it in a large saucepan with the stock, bay leaf, mace, parsley and salt. Bring the liquid to the boil over medium heat, skim the scum from the surface, then reduce the heat to low. Cover the pan and cook the chicken gently for 1 hour.

Strain the stock through a fine sieve into a large jug. Cool the stock rapidly by standing the jug in iced or very cold water for about 30 minutes. When the fat has congealed, remove it from the surface of the cooled stock.

Meanwhile, remove and discard the skin and bones from the chicken. Cut the flesh into small pieces.

Put the chicken pieces and the cooled stock into a blender or food processor and purée until very smooth. Return the soup to the saucepan.

Blend the butter and flour together to make a smooth paste. Heat the soup almost to the boil, then gradually whisk in the butter and flour. Bring to the boil, stirring all the time, then reduce the heat and simmer the soup for 10 minutes. Stir in the cream and season with pepper. Serve garnished with parsley.

SUGGESTED ACCOMPANIMENT: *raw celery sticks.*

Couscous Soup
with Harissa

HARISSA IS A HOT, SPICY MIXTURE USED TO FLAVOUR NORTH
AFRICAN DISHES; IN THIS RECIPE, SOME PIMIENTOS ARE ADDED.

Serves 8
Working time: about 40 minutes
Total time: about 1 hour and 15 minutes

Calories **360**
Protein **25g**
Cholesterol **50mg**
Total fat **15g**
Saturated fat **4g**
Sodium **750mg**

1 tbsp	olive oil	1 tbsp
15 g	unsalted butter	½ oz
1	large onion, coarsely chopped	1
½ tsp	cayenne pepper	½ tsp
½ tsp	ground cumin	½ tsp
½ tsp	cumin seeds	½ tsp
1 tsp	salt	1 tsp
½ tsp	cracked black peppercorns	½ tsp
½ tsp	ground allspice	½ tsp
4 tsp	chopped fresh thyme, or 1 tsp dried thyme	4 tsp

2 tsp	chopped fresh oregano, or ½ tsp dried oregano	2 tsp
2	bay leaves	2
2 or 3	garlic cloves, finely chopped (about 1 tbsp)	2 or 3
1.25 kg	ripe tomatoes, skinned, seeded and chopped, or 800 g (28 oz) canned tomatoes, drained and chopped	2½ lb
2 litres	unsalted chicken stock	3½ pints
1	large waxy potato, peeled and cut into 1 cm (½ inch) cubes	1
5	sticks celery, cut into 1 cm (½ inch) lengths	5
3	carrots, sliced into 5 mm (¼ inch) thick rounds	3
500 g	boneless chicken breast meat, cut into 2.5 cm (1 inch) cubes	1 lb
125 g	chorizo or other spicy sausage, cut into 1 cm (½ inch) thick rounds	4 oz
350 g	cooked and drained chick-peas	12 oz
2	courgettes, preferably 1 green and 1 yellow, each cut lengthwise into 8 strips, the strips cut into 2.5 cm (1 inch) pieces	2

▶

½	sweet green pepper, seeded, deribbed and cut lengthwise into 5 mm (¼ inch) strips	½
½	sweet red pepper, seeded, deribbed and cut lengthwise into 5 mm (¼ inch) strips	½
45 g	couscous	1½ oz
Harissa		
175 g	pimientos, drained	6 oz
1	garlic clove	1
1 tsp	Tabasco sauce	1 tsp
2 tsp	chili paste	2 tsp
2 tsp	ground cumin	2 tsp
¼ tsp	salt	¼ tsp

Heat the oil and butter in a large, heavy-bottomed saucepan over medium-high heat. Add the onion and sauté it, stirring frequently, until it is translucent — about 8 minutes. Meanwhile, combine the spices with the thyme, oregano and bay leaves in a small bowl.

Add the garlic to the onions and cook the mixture, stirring constantly, for 2 minutes more. Add the combined spices and herbs, tomatoes and stock, then increase the heat, and bring the liquid to the boil. Stir in the potato, celery and carrots. Reduce the heat, cover the pan, and simmer the mixture until the potato cubes are tender — about 20 minutes.

Add the chicken, sausage, chick-peas, courgettes, peppers and couscous, and simmer for 20 minutes.

While the soup finishes cooking, purée the harissa ingredients in a food processor or blender. Transfer the mixture to a small bowl. Serve the soup hot; allow each diner to add a dab of harissa if desired.

Crab, Fennel and Tomato Soup

Serves 4
Working time: about 45 minutes
Total time: about 2 hours

Calories **120**
Protein **13g**
Cholesterol **60mg**
Total fat **4g**
Saturated fat **1g**
Sodium **380mg**

2 tbsp	virgin olive oil	2 tbsp
1	onion, thinly sliced	1
1	small fennel bulb, trimmed, cored and thinly sliced, several stems and leaves reserved for the stock and for garnish	1
3	garlic cloves, finely chopped	3
500 g	ripe tomatoes, skinned, seeded and chopped, or 400 g (14 oz) canned tomatoes, drained and chopped	1 lb
½ tsp	salt	½ tsp
	cayenne pepper	
250 g	white crab meat	8 oz
Fish stock		
500 g	lean fish bones and trimmings	1 lb
1	large onion, thinly sliced	1
1	stick celery, thinly sliced	1
	several parsley stems (optional)	
½ litre	dry white wine	16 fl oz
8 to 10	peppercorns	8 to 10

To make the stock, pour 1.5 litres (2½ pints) of water into a large pan and add the fish bones and trimmings, onion, celery, reserved fennel stems and a few of the reserved fennel leaves, and the parsley stems if you are using them. Bring the liquid to the boil, then reduce the heat and simmer it for 15 minutes, skimming off any foam as it rises to the surface. Pour in the wine and return the liquid to the boil. Simmer the liquid for 10 minutes; add the peppercorns and simmer 5 minutes more.

Strain the fish stock into a bowl and discard the solids. Return the strained stock to the pan and boil it until it is reduced to about 1 litre (1¾ pints).

Heat the oil in another large pan over medium-low heat. Add the onion, fennel and garlic. Cover the pan and cook the vegetables, stirring occasionally, until they are soft — 10 to 15 minutes. Stir in the tomatoes, salt and a pinch of cayenne pepper. Pour in the reduced stock and bring the mixture to the boil. Reduce the heat and simmer the mixture, covered, until the fennel is very soft — about 45 minutes.

Purée the fennel-tomato mixture in batches in a blender or food processor until it is very smooth. Return the purée to the pan and add the crab meat. Cook the soup over medium-low heat until it is warmed through; garnish it with the remaining fennel leaves.

Haddock and Sweet Pepper Soup

Serves 4
Working time: about 25 minutes
Total time: about 1 hour

Calories **125**
Protein **20g**
Cholesterol **75mg**
Total fat **3g**
Saturated fat **1g**
Sodium **135mg**

500 g	haddock fillets, skinned, rinsed, patted dry, and cut into 2.5 cm (1 inch) cubes	1 lb
2 tbsp	finely chopped fresh ginger root	2 tbsp
2 tbsp	dry sherry	2 tbsp
1.5 litres	fish stock	2½ pints
4	garlic cloves, thinly sliced	4
¼ tsp	salt	¼ tsp
⅛ tsp	cayenne pepper	⅛ tsp
1	sweet red pepper, skinned, seeded, deribbed and cut into narrow strips about 2.5 cm (1 inch) long	1
1	sweet yellow pepper, skinned, seeded, deribbed and cut into narrow strips about 2.5 cm (1 inch) long	1

Place the fish cubes in a shallow dish. Scatter the ginger over them and pour in the sherry. Marinate the fish at room temperature for 30 minutes.

Meanwhile, pour the fish stock into a large, shallow pan and bring it to the boil. Stir in the sliced garlic, salt and cayenne pepper, and reduce the heat to maintain a strong simmer. Cook the mixture with the cover ajar for 30 minutes.

Add the pepper strips to the pan and cook them for 3 minutes. Pour the marinade into the pan and reduce the heat to maintain a gentle simmer. Add the fish and cook it gently until it is opaque and feels firm to the touch — about 3 minutes. Serve the hot soup immediately.

EDITOR'S NOTE: *To remove the skins from the sweet peppers, grill them on all sides until the skins blister and blacken. Cover with a damp cloth, or put them in a bowl and cover with plastic film, and leave to cool; then peel off the skins.*

Blanch the julienned carrot in ½ litre (16 fl oz) of boiling water for 2 to 3 minutes. Remove the pieces with a slotted spoon and stir them into the soup.

Put the oysters and their liquid in a small saucepan over medium heat. Gently simmer the oysters until they begin to curl at the edges — 3 to 4 minutes. Transfer the oysters and their liquid to the soup; bring the soup to a simmer (do not let it boil) and add the watercress. Simmer the soup until the watercress is wilted — 2 to 3 minutes. Sprinkle the chives and paprika over the top, if you are using them, and serve the soup immediately.

Oyster Soup with Watercress and Carrot

Serves 4
Working time: about 40 minutes
Total time: about 1 hour

Calories **245**
Protein **14g**
Cholesterol **70mg**
Total fat **8g**
Saturated fat **2g**
Sodium **365mg**

1 tbsp	safflower oil	1 tbsp
1	onion, finely chopped	1
125 g	celeriac, peeled and finely chopped	4 oz
1	potato, peeled and finely chopped	1
12.5 cl	dry white wine	4 fl oz
35 cl	fish stock	12 fl oz
¼ litre	semi-skimmed milk	8 fl oz
	cayenne pepper	
¼ tsp	white pepper	¼ tsp
1	large carrot, julienned	1
250 g	shucked oysters, liquid reserved	8 oz
90 g	watercress leaves	3 oz
2 tsp	finely cut chives (optional)	2 tsp
1 tsp	paprika, preferably Hungarian (optional)	1 tsp

Heat the oil in a large, heavy-bottomed saucepan over medium-high heat. Add the onion and celeriac and cook them until the onion is translucent — 4 to 5 minutes. Add the potato, wine and stock, then reduce the heat and simmer the mixture, covered, until the vegetables are quite soft — 15 to 20 minutes. Purée the mixture in a blender or food processor and return it to the pan. Stir in the milk along with a pinch of cayenne pepper, the white pepper and salt.

Clam and Rice Soup

Serves 4
Working time: about 35 minutes
Total time: about 50 minutes

Calories **140**
Protein **7g**
Cholesterol **25mg**
Total fat **4g**
Saturated fat **1g**
Sodium **40mg**

24	small hardshell clams, scrubbed	24
1 tbsp	virgin olive oil	1 tbsp
90 g	onion, finely chopped	3 oz
2 tsp	finely chopped garlic	2 tsp
1	small bay leaf	1
45 g	long-grain rice	1½ oz
4 tbsp	dry white wine	4 tbsp
⅛ tsp	crushed saffron threads	⅛ tsp
½ tsp	fresh lemon juice	½ tsp
1	large, ripe tomato, skinned, seeded and finely chopped	1
2 tbsp	finely chopped fresh parsley	2 tbsp

Bring 1 litre (1¾ pints) of water to the boil in a large pan. Add the clams, cover the pan tightly, and cook the clams until they open — about 5 minutes. Transfer the clams to a plate, discarding any that remain closed, and reserve the cooking liquid. When the clams are cool enough to handle, remove them from their shells. Discard the shells and set the clams aside.

Heat the oil in a heavy frying pan over medium heat. Add the onion, garlic and bay leaf, and sauté them, stirring frequently, until the onion is translucent — about 5 minutes.

Strain the clam-cooking liquid through a sieve lined with muslin, then pour the liquid back into the pan. Add the contents of the frying pan along with the rice, wine, saffron and lemon juice, and bring to the boil. Reduce the heat and cover the pan, leaving the lid ajar; simmer for 10 minutes, stirring once or twice. Add the tomato and simmer for 5 minutes more. Stir in the parsley and cook for 2 minutes longer. Return the clams to the pan and heat them through. Serve immediately.

Spinach and Fish Soup

Serves 6
Working time: about 25 minutes
Total time: about 1 hour

Calories **125**
Protein **17g**
Cholesterol **7mg**
Total fat **3g**
Saturated fat **1g**
Sodium **215mg**

2	onions, sliced	2
2	sticks celery, sliced	2
¼ tsp	ground mace	¼ tsp
½ tsp	fresh thyme, or ⅛ tsp dried thyme	½ tsp
1	bay leaf	1
	freshly ground black pepper	
1.25 litres	fish stock or unsalted chicken stock	2 pints
500 g	fillet from a firm, white-fleshed fish, such as haddock or coley, skinned and cut into 2.5 cm (1 inch) chunks	1 lb
2 tbsp	farina	2 tbsp
750 g	spinach, stemmed and washed	1½ lb
2 tbsp	double cream	2 tbsp

Put the onions, celery, mace, thyme, bay leaf and some pepper into a large pan. Pour in ¼ litre (8 fl oz) of the stock and bring the mixture to the boil. Cover the pan, reduce the heat to maintain a strong simmer, and cook

the vegetables and seasonings for 30 minutes. Remove the lid and increase the heat to medium high. Cook the mixture until the liquid has evaporated and the onions are lightly browned — about 10 minutes more.

Meanwhile, pour the remaining stock into a large shallow pan over medium-high heat and bring it to a simmer. Add the fish chunks and poach them in the simmering stock until they are opaque and feel firm to the touch — about 3 minutes. Remove the fish pieces with a slotted spoon and set them aside; reserve the poaching liquid.

Transfer ¼ litre (8 fl oz) of the poaching liquid to a small saucepan and bring it to the boil. Whisk in the farina and cook the liquid until it thickens — about 4 minutes. Set the liquid aside.

Pour the remaining poaching liquid into the pan containing the vegetables. Stir in the spinach and cook it over medium-high heat until it wilts — about 4 minutes. Purée the spinach mixture with the farina-thickened liquid in two batches in a blender, food processor or food mill. Return the soup to the pan over medium heat. Stir in the cream and the fish pieces, and cook the soup for 2 minutes. Serve immediately.

Shanghai Scallop Soup with 20 Garlic Cloves

Serves 4
Working (and total) time: about 40 minutes

Calories **230**		
Protein **25g**		
Cholesterol **45mg**		
Total fat **3g**		
Saturated fat **1g**		
Sodium **355mg**		

500 g	scallops, bright white connective tissue removed, larger scallops halved or quartered	1 lb
2 tbsp	dry sherry	2 tbsp
1 tbsp	low-sodium soy sauce or shoyu	1 tbsp
	freshly ground black pepper	
1.5 litres	unsalted chicken stock	2½ pints
20	garlic cloves, peeled	20
250 g	bok choy, leaves cut into chiffonade, stems sliced diagonally into 5 mm (¼ inch) pieces	8 oz
4 tbsp	fresh lemon juice	4 tbsp
60 g	cellophane noodles, soaked in hot water for 20 minutes, drained and cut into 2.5 cm (1 inch) lengths	2 oz
1 tbsp	chopped fresh coriander	1 tbsp

Rinse the scallops under cold water and drain. Put them into a bowl with the sherry, soy sauce and some pepper. Gently stir the scallops to coat them with the marinade; set aside.

Pour the stock into a large pan and bring it to the boil. Add the garlic cloves, reduce the heat and simmer until the cloves are tender — about 15 minutes. Then stir in the bok choy leaves and stems, and simmer for 5 minutes more. Stir in the lemon juice, noodles and scallops with their marinade. Cook until the scallops are opaque — about 1 minute. Stir in the coriander and serve.

EDITOR'S NOTE: *If bok choy (also called Chinese chard) is not available, Swiss chard can be substituted.*

Chilled Tomato and
Prawn Soup

Serves 4
Working time: about 20 minutes
Total time: about 1 hour and 20 minutes (includes chilling)

Calories **120**	½ litre	unsalted veal or chicken stock		16 fl oz
Protein **14g**	4	tomatoes, skinned, seeded, chopped		4
Cholesterol **95mg**	½	cucumber, peeled, seeded, chopped		½
Total fat **1g**	1	spring onion, trimmed and sliced		1
Saturated fat **0g**	2 tbsp	red wine vinegar		2 tbsp
Sodium **150mg**				

¼ tsp	white pepper	¼ tsp
1 tsp	Dijon mustard	1 tsp
4 to 8	drops Tabasco sauce	4 to 8
350 g	cooked peeled prawns or shrimps	12 oz
	croûtons (optional; page 9)	

Pour the stock into a serving bowl. Stir in the tomatoes, cucumber, spring onion, vinegar, pepper, mustard and Tabasco sauce. Add the prawns and stir again. Cover the bowl and refrigerate it for at least 1 hour. Serve the soup in chilled soup bowls; if you wish, garnish each portion with a few croûtons.

Mussel and Artichoke Chowder

Serves 4
Working (and total) time: about 1 hour and 15 minutes

Calories **340**
Protein **21g**
Cholesterol **80mg**
Total fat **9g**
Saturated fat **2g**
Sodium **560mg**

2	globe artichokes	2
½	lemon, juice only	½
¼ litre	dry white wine	8 fl oz
24	mussels, scrubbed and debearded	24
1 tbsp	safflower oil	1 tbsp
2	onions, finely diced	2
2 tbsp	flour	2 tbsp
½ litre	fish stock	16 fl oz
350 g	waxy potatoes, finely diced	12 oz
1	large carrot, finely diced	1
1	bay leaf	1
1	fresh thyme sprig, or ¼ tsp dried thyme	1
¼ tsp	ground mace	¼ tsp
¼ tsp	salt	¼ tsp
⅛ tsp	white pepper	⅛ tsp
½ litre	semi-skimmed milk	16 fl oz
1 tsp	paprika	1 tsp

To prepare the artichokes for cooking, first remove two or three layers of the outer leaves: pull each leaf out and down until it snaps off at its base; stop when you reach the tender inner leaves. Cut off the top of the artichoke about 4 cm (1½ inches) above the base. Discard the outer leaves.

Cut off the stem flush with the base, then peel around the base in a spiral motion to pare away the dark green bases of the leaves. Turn the artichoke over. With the same spiral motion you used to cut off the leaf bases, trim the light green parts from the upper half of the artichoke. Using a sturdy teaspoon, scrape out the choke — the densely packed, fibrous centre — and discard it. To preserve its colour, drop the bottom into water mixed with the lemon juice. Prepare the other artichoke in the same way.

Pour the wine into a large, non-reactive pan over medium heat and bring it to a simmer. Add the mussels and cover the pan. Steam the mussels, shaking the pan a few times, until they open — about 2 minutes. Transfer the opened mussels to a bowl; discard any that remain closed. Reserve the wine.

Rinse the pan and heat the oil in it over medium heat. Add the onions and cook them, stirring, until they are ▶

translucent — about 4 minutes. Whisk in the flour, then the reserved wine, forming a paste. Slowly pour in the stock, whisking constantly. Bring the liquid to the boil and reduce the heat to maintain a simmer. Simmer the liquid until it is thickened — about 5 minutes.

Remove the mussels from their shells, working over a bowl to catch any of their juices. Line a sieve with muslin and strain the juices through it into the onion mixture. Add the potatoes, carrot, bay leaf, thyme, mace, salt and pepper. Simmer the vegetables, partially covered, for about 10 minutes. Discard the bay leaf and the thyme sprig if you used it, and continue cooking the vegetables until the potatoes and carrot

are tender — about 5 minutes more.

While the potatoes and carrot are cooking, pour 1 litre (1¾ pints) of water into a non-reactive saucepan. Bring the water to the boil and add the artichoke bottoms; reduce the heat and simmer the bottoms until they can be easily pierced through with the tip of a sharp knife — about 15 minutes. Drain the bottoms; when they are cool enough to handle, cut them into small dice.

Add the diced artichoke to the soup. Stir in the milk and the mussels, and cook the chowder over low heat until the mussels are heated through — 3 to 4 minutes. Sprinkle the chowder with the paprika just before serving.

Fish Soup
with Red Pepper Sauce

Serves 6
Working (and total) time: about 45 minutes

Calories **205**
Protein **17g**
Cholesterol **35mg**
Total fat **9g**
Saturated fat **1g**
Sodium **160mg**

1.5 litres	fish stock	2½ pints
3	large leeks, green tops discarded, white parts split, washed thoroughly to remove all grit, and thinly sliced	3
250 g	finely shredded Savoy cabbage	8 oz
2	ripe tomatoes, skinned, seeded and chopped	2
500 g	fillet from a firm, white-fleshed fish such as cod, rinsed and cut into 2.5 cm (1 inch) chunks	1 lb
4 tbsp	freshly grated pecorino cheese	4 tbsp
	Red pepper sauce	
2	wholemeal bread slices, crusts removed	2
1	sweet red pepper, seeded, deribbed and chopped	1
2	large garlic cloves, chopped	2
⅛ tsp	cayenne pepper	⅛ tsp
3 tbsp	virgin olive oil	3 tbsp

To prepare the red pepper sauce, first put the bread slices into a bowl and pour in enough water to cover them. Soak the slices for 10 minutes, then squeeze out the water and transfer the bread to a food processor. Add the red pepper, garlic and cayenne pepper, and

purée the mixture. With the machine still running, dribble in the olive oil; the resulting sauce should be thick. Set the sauce aside.

For the soup, pour the stock into a large pan and bring it to the boil. Add the leeks, cabbage and tomatoes, then reduce the heat and simmer the vegetables until they are tender — about 10 minutes. Add the fish and cook the soup until the fish is firm and opaque — about 3 minutes. Pass the cheese and the red pepper sauce in separate bowls.

Oyster Soup with Leeks

Serves 6
Working (and total) time: about 45 minutes

Calories **125**
Protein **8g**
Cholesterol **50mg**
Total fat **5g**
Saturated fat **3g**
Sodium **115mg**

15 g	unsalted butter	½ oz
2	large leeks, trimmed, split, washed thoroughly to remove all grit, and thinly sliced	2
2 tsp	fresh thyme, or ½ tsp dried thyme	2 tsp
3	garlic cloves, finely chopped	3
12.5 cl	dry white wine	4 fl oz
60 cl	fish stock	1 pint
⅛ tsp	salt	⅛ tsp
	freshly ground black pepper	
250 g	freshly shucked large oysters	8 oz
4 tbsp	single cream	4 tbsp

Melt the butter in a large, heavy-bottomed saucepan over medium-high heat. Add the leeks and thyme, then cover the pan and cook the leeks, stirring them several times, for 10 minutes.

Add the garlic and wine; continue cooking, stirring frequently, until the wine evaporates — about 5 minutes. Pour in the stock, then add the salt and some pepper, and simmer the mixture for 10 minutes.

While the stock is simmering, set aside 12 of the oysters. Purée the remaining oysters with their liquid in a food processor or blender.

Remove the pan from the heat, then whisk in the oyster purée and the cream. Set the pan over very low heat and cook the soup just long enough to heat it through — about 3 minutes. Place two of the reserved oysters in each of six heated soup plates. Pour the soup over the oysters and serve at once.

Hot and Sweet Soup with Seafood Dumplings

Serves 8
Working time: about 1 hour
Total time: about 1 hour and 15 minutes

Calories **135**
Protein **17g**
Cholesterol **75mg**
Total fat **3g**
Saturated fat **1g**
Sodium **240mg**

250 g	finely chopped lean pork	8 oz
250 g	fresh prawns, peeled, deveined if necessary, and finely chopped	8 oz
250 g	white crab meat, picked over	8 oz
2	spring onions, trimmed and finely chopped	2
1½ tsp	finely chopped fresh ginger root	1½ tsp
1	egg white, beaten	1
2 litres	unsalted chicken stock	3½ pints
2 tsp	sweet chili sauce, or 1 tsp crushed hot red pepper flakes mixed with 2 tsp golden syrup and 1 tsp vinegar	2 tsp
12.5 cl	fresh lemon juice	4 fl oz
250 g	small cantaloupe melon balls	8 oz
¼ tsp	salt	¼ tsp

Combine the pork, prawns, crab meat, spring onions, ginger and egg white in a large bowl. Shape heaped teaspoonfuls of the mixture into dumplings about 2.5 cm (1 inch) in diameter, moistening your palms from time to time to keep the mixture from sticking to them.

Pour the stock into a large pan and bring it to the boil. Reduce the heat to maintain a strong simmer and add the chili sauce or pepper-flake mixture and 4 table-spoons of the lemon juice. Gently drop half of the dumplings into the hot liquid and simmer them for 5 minutes. Remove the dumplings with a slotted spoon and set them aside. Drop the remaining dumplings into the liquid and simmer them for 5 minutes. When the second batch is done, return the first batch of dumplings to the pan. Heat the dumplings through, then add the melon balls, the salt and the remaining lemon juice. Serve the soup in individual bowls.

A Fine Kettle of Fish

Serves 8
Working (and total) time: about 45 minutes

Calories **200**
Protein **25g**
Cholesterol **95mg**
Total fat **6g**
Saturated fat **1g**
Sodium **190mg**

1.5 litres	fish stock or unsalted chicken stock	2½ pints
¼ litre	dry white wine	8 fl oz
2 tbsp	virgin olive oil	2 tbsp
4	spring onions, trimmed and finely chopped	4
16	small hardshell clams, scrubbed	16
16	mussels, scrubbed and debearded	16
16	fresh prawns, peeled, deveined if necessary	16
750 g	redfish (or Norway haddock) fillets, cut into 2.5 cm (1 inch) cubes	1½ lb
750 g	ripe tomatoes, skinned, seeded and coarsely chopped, or 400 g (14 oz) canned tomatoes, drained and coarsely chopped	1½ lb
3 tbsp	finely cut chives	3 tbsp
1 tbsp	fresh thyme, or ¾ tsp dried thyme	1 tbsp
1	lemon, grated rind only	1
⅛ tsp	cayenne pepper	⅛ tsp
⅛ tsp	crushed saffron threads	⅛ tsp
4 tbsp	finely chopped fresh parsley	4 tbsp

Pour the stock, wine and oil into a large, non-reactive pan. Add the spring onions and bring the liquid to the boil. Add the clams and mussels and cook them, partially covered, for 2 minutes. Remove the opened clams and mussels and set them aside. Partially cover the pan again and cook the mixture for 2 minutes more. Remove and set aside the opened clams and mussels; discard any that remain closed. Strain the cooking liquid into a bowl through a sieve lined with muslin. Rinse the pan and return the strained liquid to it.

Add the prawns and fish to the pan and return the liquid to the boil. Stir in the tomatoes, chives, thyme, lemon rind, cayenne pepper, saffron and parsley. Add the reserved clams and mussels and remove the pan from the heat. Let the soup stand for 5 minutes so that the flavours may meld.

Divide the clams, mussels and prawns between eight bowls. Ladle some fish and broth into each, and serve.

Thai Prawn Soup with Lemon Grass

Serves 6 as a first course
Working time: about 30 minutes
Total time: about 45 minutes

Calories **50**
Protein **6g**
Cholesterol **40mg**
Total fat **0g**
Saturated fat **0g**
Sodium **180mg**

2 tsp	safflower oil	2 tsp
250 g	fresh prawns, peeled, deveined if necessary and halved lengthwise, the shells reserved	8 oz
60 cl	unsalted chicken stock	1 pint
2	stalks lemon grass, the root ends and woody tops trimmed off, the stalks cut into 2.5 cm (1 inch) long pieces, or 1 tsp grated lemon rind	2
4 tbsp	fresh lime juice	4 tbsp
½ tsp	sambal oelek or crushed hot red pepper flakes	½ tsp
2 tsp	fish sauce	2 tsp
6	paper-thin slices of lime for garnish	6
	fresh coriander leaves for garnish (optional)	

Heat the oil in a heavy pan over medium heat. Add the prawn shells and cook them, stirring, until they turn bright pink — about 1 minute. Add the stock, 60 cl (1 pint) of water and the lemon grass if you are using it. (If you are substituting lemon rind, do not add it yet.) Bring the liquid to the boil, then reduce the heat to medium low, cover the pan, and simmer the mixture for 5 minutes. Turn off the heat and let the liquid stand for 15 minutes.

Strain the stock into a bowl. Discard the solids and return the liquid to the pan. Bring the liquid to a simmer and add the lime juice, crushed red pepper flakes, fish sauce and prawns. If you are using lemon rind, add it now. Cook the soup until the prawns are opaque — about 1 minute. To serve, ladle the soup into bowls and garnish each one with a lime slice and, if you like, some coriander leaves.

EDITOR'S NOTE: *Fish sauce (see glossary) is available in well-stocked supermarkets; fresh lemon grass and sambal oelek may be purchased in Asian grocery shops.*

Sweetcorn, Scallop and Fettuccine Soup

Serves 4
Working (and total) time: about 25 minutes

Calories **330**	350 g	scallops, bright white connective tissue removed, large scallops cut in half horizontally	12 oz
Protein **21g**			
Cholesterol **45mg**			
Total fat **9g**	⅛ tsp	white pepper	⅛ tsp
Saturated fat **3g**	½ tsp	salt	½ tsp
Sodium **385mg**	¼ litre	semi-skimmed milk	8 fl oz
	1 litre	fish stock	1¾ pints
	125 g	spinach fettuccine	4 oz
	175 g	frozen sweetcorn kernels	6 oz
	1 tbsp	safflower oil	1 tbsp
	15 g	unsalted butter	½ oz
	2 tbsp	finely chopped shallot	2 tbsp
	12.5 cl	dry white wine	4 fl oz
½ tsp	chopped fresh thyme, or ⅛ tsp dried thyme		½ tsp

Rinse the scallops under cold running water and drain them. Season the scallops with the pepper and ¼ teaspoon of the salt, and set them aside.

Pour the milk and stock into a large pan. Sprinkle in the remaining salt and bring the liquid to the boil. Add the fettuccine and sweetcorn. Cover the pan until the liquid returns to the boil, then cook until the pasta is *al dente* — about 8 minutes.

While the fettuccine and sweetcorn are cooking, heat the oil and butter together in a heavy frying pan over medium-high heat. Add the scallops and sauté them for 30 seconds on each side. Add the shallot and cook, stirring, for 1 minute. Pour in the wine, then add the thyme and cook for 1 minute more.

When the pasta is ready, combine it with the scallop mixture and serve at once.

Vietnamese Crab and Asparagus Soup

Serves 6
Working (and total) time: about 30 minutes

Calories **130**
Protein **16g**
Cholesterol **60mg**
Total fat **5g**
Saturated fat **1g**
Sodium **390mg**

4	dried Asian mushrooms, covered with ¼ litre (8 fl oz) of boiling water and soaked for 20 minutes	4
1 tbsp	safflower oil	1 tbsp
3	spring onions, trimmed, the white parts chopped, the green tops thinly sliced crosswise	3
3	garlic cloves, finely chopped	3
1.25 litres	unsalted chicken stock	2 pints
250 g	fresh asparagus, trimmed and cut diagonally into 2.5 cm (1 inch) pieces	8 oz
1 tbsp	fish sauce or low-sodium soy sauce	1 tbsp
	freshly ground black pepper	
500 g	white crab meat, picked over	1 lb
2 tbsp	chopped fresh coriander, plus several whole leaves for garnish	2 tbsp

Strain the mushroom-soaking liquid through a fine sieve lined with muslin and set the liquid aside. Cut off and discard the stems; slice the caps.

Heat the oil in a heavy pan over medium-high heat. Add the white spring onion parts and the garlic; sauté them, stirring often, for 1 minute. Pour in the mushroom-soaking liquid and the stock, then add the mushroom caps and bring the mixture to the boil. Add the asparagus, the fish sauce or soy sauce, the green spring onion tops and some pepper. Return the liquid to the boil, then reduce the heat to maintain a simmer. Cook the asparagus pieces until they are barely tender — about 3 minutes.

Add the crab meat and stir in the chopped coriander. Simmer the soup for 2 minutes more to heat the crab through. Garnish the soup with the coriander leaves before serving.

Fruit soups, long savoured in central Europe, can be a welcome addition to the menu. Here are three, made with pears, melon and orange, and peaches.

Gingery Pear Soup

Serves 4 as a first course
Working time: about 10 minutes
Total time: about 30 minutes

Calories **150**
Protein **4g**
Cholesterol **6mg**
Total fat **6g**
Saturated fat **1g**
Sodium **210mg**

1 tbsp	safflower oil	1 tbsp
2 tbsp	finely chopped fresh ginger root	2 tbsp
1 tbsp	finely chopped shallot	1 tbsp
4 tbsp	pear brandy (optional)	4 tbsp
500 g	pears, quartered, cored and sliced into thin wedges	1 lb
½ litre	unsalted chicken stock	16 fl oz
¼ tsp	salt	¼ tsp
¼ litre	semi-skimmed milk	8 fl oz
4	parsley sprigs for garnish	4

Heat the oil in a large, heavy-bottomed saucepan over medium heat. Add the ginger and shallot and cook them, stirring, until the shallot is translucent — 2 to 3 minutes. Pour in the brandy if you are using it, and cook the mixture until the liquid is nearly evaporated — about 3 minutes more.

Add the pears, stock and salt. Reduce the heat and simmer the mixture, partially covered, until the pears are translucent and soft — 15 to 20 minutes. Remove a few pear slices and set them aside for garnish.

Purée the contents of the pan in a food processor or blender. Return the purée to the pan, stir in the milk and warm the soup over low heat, taking care that it does not boil. Serve the soup immediately, garnished with the reserved pear slices and the parsley sprigs.

Golden Gazpacho

Serves 6 as a first course
Working time: about 15 minutes
Total time: about 1 hour and 15 minutes (includes chilling)

Calories **75**
Protein **3g**
Cholesterol **1mg**
Total fat **1g**
Saturated fat **0g**
Sodium **20mg**

1	ripe melon, peeled, seeded and diced	
2	garlic cloves, peeled	
2	sweet yellow peppers, seeded, deribbed and quartered	
½ to 1	hot green chili pepper, seeded and deribbed (caution, page 95)	½ to 1
30 g	fresh coriander leaves	1 o.
1	orange, peeled and quartered, rind of one quarter reserved	
35 cl	fresh orange juice	12 fl o.
3	spring onions, white parts only	
1½ tbsp	fresh lime juice	1½ tbsp
12.5 cl	plain low-fat yogurt	4 fl o.
12	fresh coriander leaves for garnish	12

Place all the ingredients except the yogurt in a food processor and purée the mixture. Add the yogurt and operate the machine in short bursts until the yogurt is mixed in. Transfer the soup to a bowl or jar, cover it tightly, and refrigerate it for at least 1 hour.

Garnish each serving with the coriander leaves.

EDITOR'S NOTE: *In the event that sweet yellow peppers cannot be found, use sweet red peppers instead.*

Peach Soup Flambé

Serves 4 as a first course
Working (and total) time: about 1 hour

Calories **185**
Protein **2g**
Cholesterol **5mg**
Total fat **3g**
Saturated fat **2g**
Sodium **6mg**

1 kg	ripe peaches or nectarines, washed	2 lb
4 tbsp	fresh lemon juice	4 tbsp
1 tbsp	honey	1 tbsp
1 tsp	chopped fresh rosemary, or ¼ tsp dried rosemary	1 tsp
4 tsp	sugar	4 tsp
4 tbsp	soured cream	4 tbsp
3 tbsp	cognac or Armagnac	3 tbsp

Pour 2 litres (3½ pints) of water into a large pan. Bring the water to the boil, then add the peaches and cook them until their skins loosen — 5 to 15 minutes, depending on their ripeness. Using a slotted spoon, remove the peaches and set them aside to cool. Pour off all but 35 cl (12 fl oz) of the cooking water.

When the peaches are cool enough to handle, peel them, then cut them in half and remove the stones.

Discard the skins and stones; return the peach halves to the pan. Add the lemon juice, honey, rosemary and 3 teaspoons of the sugar, and bring the mixture to the boil. Reduce the heat and simmer the peaches, stirring frequently, for 15 minutes.

Purée the mixture in batches in a blender, a food processor or a food mill. Pour the purée back into the pan and reheat it slowly over low heat, stirring occasionally, for about 10 minutes. Stir in 2 tablespoons of the soured cream.

Transfer the soup to a warmed serving bowl. Mix the remaining soured cream with the remaining sugar, then spoon the mixture on to the centre of the soup. Gently spoon the cognac or Armagnac round the soured cream, taking care that the brandy floats on the surface of the soup. Dim the lights, ignite the brandy, and serve the soup with the flames dancing.

88

2 Asian-inspired, this beef stew with water chestnuts and squash takes its character from the tangerine juice and peel it includes (recipe, page 101).

Stew's Ever-Constant Magic

Is there anything so simple or so nourishing as a stew? Conjuring up the memory of a Provençal beef stew simmering on his grandmother's kitchen stove, French author Pierre Huguenin recalled that it sounded "like a little bubbling spring" as it cooked. "Since midday," he wrote, "it had been murmuring gently, giving out sweet smells. Thyme, rosemary, bay leaves, spices, the wine of the marinade and the meat were becoming transformed under the magic wand which is the fire, into a delicious whole."

In the alchemy that is stew-making, almost any ingredient can be transmuted into something special. This section endeavours to delight by presenting a broad repertoire of stews based on vegetables, fish and meat. Many of the recipes have an international flavour: the rabbit stew on page 105, for example, which includes sweetcorn, broad beans and potatoes, has its origins in the American south. Other dishes announce their debt to ethnic cuisines by calling for spices and seasonings in exotic combinations: the Java lamb curry on page 99 draws on ginger, cloves, sweet red pepper and tamarind to give it the savour of the tropical island that inspired it. The plaice curry on page 125 features the turmeric, cardamom and mace characteristic of Indian cooking.

Wherever fattier cuts of meat are called for, the stews are degreased; when lean cuts are used, the preparation times are pared back to guarantee succulence — abbreviating, into the bargain, the cook's time in the kitchen. The sauerbraten stew with crystallized ginger on page 113 not only uses lean beef but shortcuts the marinating time of a traditional sauerbraten by at least two days. The beef is cut up into small pieces and is sautéed with the ginger; a hot marinade is then poured over all. Because the beef pieces present multiple surfaces, they need only brief steaming to absorb flavour.

During the time it simmers, a stew may be left practically unattended, freeing the cook to prepare the rest of the meal. In the meantime, as the liquid in the pan reduces, it works a final bit of magic, turning itself into a sauce that demands no further sorcery but to be skimmed of any surface fat before serving.

Sherried Vegetable Potpourri

Serves 6
Working time: about 30 minutes
Total time: about 1 hour

Calories **115**
Protein **3g**
Cholesterol **0mg**
Total fat **3g**
Saturated fat **0g**
Sodium **165mg**

1 tbsp	safflower oil	1 tbsp
30 g	shallots, thinly sliced	1 oz
2	garlic cloves, finely chopped	2
¼ litre	dry sherry	8 fl oz
1 tbsp	chopped fresh thyme, or ¾ tsp dried thyme	1 tbsp
1	carrot, cut into 2 cm (¾ inch) pieces	1
1	small swede, peeled and cut into 2 cm (¾ inch) cubes	1
150 g	cauliflower florets	5 oz
2	courgettes (preferably 1 green and 1 yellow), halved lengthwise and cut into 2 cm (¾ inch) thick pieces	2
1	small aubergine, cut into 2 cm (¾ inch) cubes	1
1	sweet red pepper, seeded, deribbed and cut into 2 cm (¾ inch) squares	1
400 g	canned tomatoes, seeded and coarsely chopped, with their juice	14 oz
30 g	red cabbage, coarsely shredded	1 oz
1 tsp	celery seeds	1 tsp
⅜ tsp	salt	⅜ tsp
	freshly ground black pepper	

Pour the oil into a large, heavy-bottomed pan over medium heat. Cook the shallots in the hot oil, stirring frequently, until they are golden — about 7 minutes. Add the garlic and continue cooking for 1 minute. Pour in all but 1 tablespoon of the sherry; add the thyme and bring the mixture to the boil, then cook it for 2 minutes more.

Put a steamer into a large saucepan; pour in about ½ litre (16 fl oz) of water and bring it to the boil. Add the carrot, swede and cauliflower and steam them, covered, for 7 minutes. Add the courgettes, aubergine and red pepper; steam these for 3 minutes more. Transfer the steamed vegetables to the pan containing the shallots; do not discard the liquid.

Add 12.5 cl (4 fl oz) of the liquid to the pan along with the tomatoes and their juice. Stir in the shredded red cabbage, celery seeds, salt and some pepper; bring the stew to a simmer and cook it, uncovered, for 10 minutes. Stir in the reserved tablespoon of sherry just before serving.

Vegetable Stew with Okra

Serves 4
Working time: about 25 minutes
Total time: about 45 minutes

Calories **195**
Protein **5g**
Cholesterol **0mg**
Total fat **8g**
Saturated fat **1g**
Sodium **115mg**

2 tbsp	safflower oil	2 tbsp
1	large sweet red pepper, seeded, deribbed and cut into 2 cm (¾ inch) squares	1
350 g	pearl onions, peeled and trimmed	12 oz
2	garlic cloves, finely chopped	2
½ litre	unsalted vegetable or chicken stock	16 fl oz
350 g	aubergine, cut into 2 cm (¾ inch) cubes	12 oz
1	yellow squash or courgette, cut into 2 cm (¾ inch) chunks	1
125 g	fresh okra (8 to 10 pods), washed and sliced into 2 cm (¾ inch) thick rounds	4 oz
750 g	ripe tomatoes, skinned, seeded and coarsely chopped, or 400 g (14 oz) canned tomatoes, chopped, with their juice	1½ lb
350 g	butternut squash or pumpkin, peeled, seeded and julienned	12 oz
1½ tbsp	chopped fresh basil, or 1 tbsp dried basil	1½ tbsp
2 tsp	Dijon mustard	2 tsp
1 tsp	paprika, preferably Hungarian	1 tsp
⅛ tsp	salt	⅛ tsp
	freshly ground black pepper	
	cayenne pepper	

Heat 1 tablespoon of the safflower oil in a large, heavy-bottomed saucepan over medium heat. Add the red pepper and pearl onions and cook them, stirring occasionally, until the pepper begins to soften and the onions have coloured slightly — about 5 minutes. Stir in the garlic and cook for 30 seconds. Pour in the stock and bring it to a brisk simmer. Reduce the heat and simmer the vegetables for 10 minutes.

While the vegetables are simmering, heat the remaining oil in a large, heavy frying pan over medium-high heat. Add the aubergine, courgette and okra, and sauté them until they begin to soften — about 3 minutes. Stir in the tomatoes, squash and basil, and cook them for 3 minutes. Add this mixture to the vegetables simmering in the pan. Stir in the mustard, paprika, salt, some black pepper and a pinch of cayenne pepper. Cook the stew until all of the vegetables are tender — about 5 minutes. Serve at once.

Sweet Potato Stew

Serves 6 as a side dish
Working time: about 40 minutes
Total time: about 1 hour

Calories **235**
Protein **5g**
Cholesterol **10mg**
Total fat **5g**
Saturated fat **3g**
Sodium **340mg**

750 g	sweet potatoes	1½ lb
30 g	unsalted butter	1 oz
30 g	shallot, finely chopped	1 oz
1 tsp	mustard seeds	1 tsp
350 g	swedes, peeled, sliced 1 cm (½ inch) thick and cut into 2.5 cm (1 inch) squares	12 oz
250 g	young turnips, peeled, sliced 1 cm (½ inch) thick and cut into 2.5 cm (1 inch) squares	8 oz
350 g	celeriac, peeled, sliced 1 cm (½ inch) thick and cut into 2.5 cm (1 inch) squares	12 oz
¾ litre	unsalted veal, chicken or vegetable stock	1¼ pints
2 tbsp	fresh lemon juice	2 tbsp
½ tsp	salt	½ tsp
70 g	parsley sprigs (about 1 bunch)	2½ oz

Preheat the oven to 200°C (400°F or Mark 6). Prick each sweet potato with a fork. Bake the sweet potatoes until they are tender — about 45 minutes.

Meanwhile, melt the butter in a large, non-reactive, heavy-bottomed saucepan over medium-low heat. Stir in the shallot and mustard seeds, and cook them for 1 minute. Add the swedes, turnips and celeriac; continue cooking, stirring frequently, for 10 minutes. Pour in 35 cl (12 fl oz) of the stock and the lemon juice; sprinkle in ¼ teaspoon of the salt. Bring the mixture to the boil, cover the pan and set it aside.

When the sweet potatoes are cooked, halve them lengthwise and spoon their flesh into a food processor or blender. Purée them with the remaining stock and salt. Stir the purée and the parsley into the mixture in the pan. Cook the stew over medium-low heat until it is heated through — about 3 minutes.

Vegetable Stew, East Indian-Style

Serves 6
Working time: about 1½ hours
Total time: about 2 hours

Calories **295**
Protein **16g**
Cholesterol **10mg**
Total fat **13g**
Saturated fat **3g**
Sodium **330mg**

1 tbsp	safflower oil	1 tbsp
15 g	unsalted butter	½ oz
1 tbsp	finely chopped fresh ginger root	1 tbsp
1	medium onion, thinly sliced	1
2	bunches of spring onions, trimmed and cut diagonally into 5 cm (2 inch) lengths	2
3	garlic cloves, thinly sliced	3
1 tsp	crushed saffron threads	1 tsp
½ tsp	ground cardamom	½ tsp
½ tsp	ground cumin	½ tsp
½ tsp	ground cinnamon	½ tsp
¼ tsp	salt	¼ tsp
	freshly ground black pepper	
2 litres	unsalted chicken or vegetable stock	3½ pints
2	potatoes, cut into 1 cm (½ inch) pieces	2
6	sticks celery, julienned	6
2	carrots, julienned	2
4 tsp	cornflour	4 tsp
150 g	stemmed spring greens, chopped	5 oz
150 g	stemmed kale, chopped	5 oz
125 g	stemmed spinach, chopped	4 oz
500 g	firm tofu (bean curd), cut into 2.5 cm (1 inch) cubes	1 lb
45 g	unsalted pistachios, shelled and chopped	1½ oz
Cucumber-yogurt sauce		
4 tbsp	plain low-fat yogurt	4 tbsp
250 g	cucumber, peeled, seeded and finely chopped	8 oz
1	tomato, skinned, seeded, finely chopped	1
1 tbsp	chopped onion	1 tbsp
2 tbsp	chopped fresh coriander	2 tbsp
⅛ tsp	salt	⅛ tsp
¼ tsp	ground cumin	¼ tsp

To prepare the sauce, combine the yogurt, cucumber, tomato, onion, coriander, salt and cumin in a bowl. Cover the bowl with plastic film and refrigerate it.

Heat the oil and butter in a large, heavy-bottomed pan over medium heat. Add the ginger and cook, stirring, for 1 minute. Add the onion and spring onions, cover the pan, and cook, stirring occasionally, for 5 minutes. Add the garlic, saffron, cardamom, cumin, cinnamon, salt and a generous grinding of pepper; cook the mixture, stirring constantly, for 2 minutes.

Pour in all but 12.5 cl (4 fl oz) of the stock and add the potatoes. Simmer, covered, for 10 minutes. Add the celery and carrots, and continue simmering until the potatoes are tender — 10 to 15 minutes. Mix the cornflour with the remaining stock and stir into the stew. Simmer until it thickens — about 3 minutes.

Stir in the spring greens, kale and spinach, and simmer until they are tender — 5 to 8 minutes. Add the tofu; pass the sauce and pistachios separately.

Chunky Beef Chili

Serves 8
Working time: about 1 hour
Total time: about 4 hours

Calories **230**
Protein **27g**
Cholesterol **75mg**
Total fat **10g**
Saturated fat **3g**
Sodium **460mg**

2	large dried mild chili peppers, stemmed, seeded and quartered	2
2	fresh hot green chili peppers, stemmed, seeded and coarsely chopped (caution, page 95)	2
2 tbsp	safflower oil	2 tbsp
1 kg	beef chuck or braising steak, trimmed of fat and cut into 1 cm (½ inch) chunks	2 lb
2	large onions, finely chopped	2
2	sticks celery, finely chopped	2
2	garlic cloves, finely chopped	2
2 tbsp	finely chopped fresh ginger root	2 tbsp
1 tbsp	ground cumin	1 tbsp
1 tbsp	dried oregano	1 tbsp
¼ tsp	cayenne pepper	¼ tsp
¼ tsp	freshly ground black pepper	¼ tsp
1 tbsp	plain flour	1 tbsp
400 g	canned tomatoes, coarsely chopped, with their juice	14 oz
1	bay leaf	1
1½ tsp	salt	1½ tsp
½ tsp	grated orange rind	½ tsp

Put the dried mild chilies into a small saucepan; pour in ½ litre (16 fl oz) of water and boil the liquid for 5 minutes. Turn off the heat and let the chilies soften for 5 minutes. Transfer them to a blender or food processor with 12.5 cl (4 fl oz) of their soaking liquid; reserve the remaining liquid. Add the fresh chili peppers and purée until the mixture is very smooth. Strain the purée through a sieve into the reserved soaking liquid, rubbing the solids through with a spoon.

Heat ½ tablespoon of the oil in a large, non-stick or heavy frying pan over medium-high heat. Add about one quarter of the beef chunks and cook them, turning the pieces frequently, until they are browned all over — approximately 8 minutes. Transfer the browned beef to a large, heavy-bottomed pan. Brown the rest of the meat the same way, using all but ½ tablespoon of the remaining oil in the process.

Add the last ½ tablespoon of oil to the frying pan along with the onions, celery and garlic. Sauté the vegetables for 5 minutes, stirring frequently. Stir in the ginger, cumin, oregano, cayenne pepper and black pepper, and cook the mixture for 1 minute. Add the flour and cook for 1 minute more, stirring constantly. Transfer the mixture to the pan.

Pour the reserved chili mixture and ½ litre (16 fl oz) of water into the pan. Stir in the tomatoes and their juice along with the bay leaf, salt and orange rind. Cook the mixture, uncovered, over very low heat until the meat is tender — 2½ to 3 hours. (Do not allow the mixture to boil or the meat will toughen.) If the chili begins to get too thick, add water, 12.5 cl (4 fl oz) at a time, until it reaches the desired consistency.

EDITOR'S NOTE: *Black beans or kidney beans make an excellent accompaniment to this orange-scented chili.*

Chili Peppers — a Cautionary Note

Both dried and fresh hot chilies should be handled with care. Their flesh and seeds contain volatile oils that can make skin tingle and cause eyes to burn. Rubber gloves offer protection — but the cook should still be careful not to touch the face, lips or eyes when working with chilies.

Soaking fresh chili peppers in cold, salted water for an hour will remove some of their fire. If canned chilies are substituted for fresh ones, they should be rinsed in cold water in order to eliminate as much of the brine used to preserve them as possible.

Lentil-Sausage Stew

Serves 6
Working time: about 15 minutes
Total time: about 1 hour

Calories **185**
Protein **12g**
Cholesterol **10mg**
Total fat **6g**
Saturated fat **2g**
Sodium **515mg**

90 g	chorizo sausage, skinned, sliced into very thin rounds, all but a few of the rounds cut into thin strips	3 oz
1	large onion, very finely chopped	1
300 g	lentils, picked over	10 oz
¾ litre	unsalted brown or chicken stock	1¼ pints
1	large carrot, sliced into thin rounds	1
2	sticks celery, thinly sliced	2
1 tbsp	chopped fresh basil, or 2 tsp dried basil	1 tbsp
½ tsp	salt	½ tsp
	freshly ground black pepper	

Cook the chorizo rounds and strips in a large, heavy pan over medium-low heat for 3 minutes. Remove the rounds and set aside. Add the onion and continue cooking until the onion is translucent — about 6 minutes.

Rinse the lentils under cold running water and add them to the pan along with the stock and ¾ litre (1¼ pints) of water. Bring the liquid to a simmer and cook the mixture, covered, until the lentils are soft — about 35 minutes. Add the carrot, celery, basil, salt and some pepper; simmer the stew, covered, until the carrot rounds are tender — 7 to 10 minutes. Garnish the stew with the reserved chorizo rounds; serve at once.

Turkey Stew with Mediterranean Vegetables

Serves 4
Working time: about 40 minutes
Total time: about 2 hours

Calories **335**
Protein **33g**
Cholesterol **85mg**
Total fat **15g**
Saturated fat **3g**
Sodium **225mg**

1 kg	turkey drumsticks	2 lb
2	onions, sliced	2
1	whole garlic bulb, cut in half horizontally	1
1 tsp	fresh thyme, or ¼ tsp dried thyme	1 tsp
1	bay leaf	1
500 g	aubergine, sliced into 1 cm (½ inch) thick rounds, each round cut into 8 wedges	1 lb
2 tbsp	virgin olive oil	2 tbsp
500 g	courgettes, trimmed and sliced into 2.5 cm (1 inch) thick rounds, rounds halved	1 lb
1 tbsp	chopped fresh oregano or parsley	1 tbsp
	Red pepper sauce	
1	sweet red pepper, seeded and chopped	1
4	garlic cloves, crushed	4
1 tbsp	chopped fresh oregano, or 1 tsp dried oregano	1 tbsp
¼ tsp	salt	¼ tsp

Put the drumsticks, onions, garlic-bulb halves, thyme and bay leaf into a large pan. Pour in enough water (about 2 litres/3½ pints) to cover the ingredients; bring the liquid to the boil over medium-high heat. Cover the pan with the lid slightly ajar, then reduce the heat and simmer until the turkey is tender — about 1 hour.

While the turkey is cooking, prepare the aubergine. Preheat the oven to 230°C (450°F or Mark 8). In a baking dish, toss the aubergine with the oil to coat the pieces. Bake the aubergine until it is lightly browned — about 15 minutes. Set it aside.

To make the sauce, transfer 12.5 cl (4 fl oz) of the simmering broth to a small saucepan over medium-low heat. Add the red pepper, bring the liquid to a simmer, and cover the pan. Cook the pepper until it is tender — 7 to 8 minutes. Put the pepper pieces and broth in a blender with the garlic, oregano and salt. Purée the mixture until a smooth sauce results. Return the sauce to the pan and set it aside.

When the turkey is tender, remove the drumsticks from the broth and set them aside. Cook the broth over high heat until only about ½ litre (16 fl oz) of liquid remain — 15 to 20 minutes.

While the broth is reducing, remove the meat from the drumsticks; discard the skin and tendons. Cut the meat into 2.5 cm (l inch) pieces. Strain the reduced broth through a fine sieve into a bowl. Discard the solids; then degrease the broth (box, page 55).

Return the broth to the pan and bring it to the boil. Add the courgettes, cover the pan and cook the courgettes until they are tender — about 5 minutes. Add the turkey, aubergine and oregano; continue cooking just long enough to heat them through. Reheat the sauce. Ladle the stew into deep plates and garnish with a dollop of the sauce before serving.

Chicken Gumbo

Serves 6
Working time: about 35 minutes
Total time: about 1 hour and 10 minutes

Calories **295**
Protein **29g**
Cholesterol **80mg**
Total fat **12g**
Saturated fat **3g**
Sodium **315mg**

1 tbsp	finely chopped garlic	1 tbsp
1 tbsp	chopped fresh thyme, or ¾ tsp dried thyme	1 tbsp
1 tsp	dry mustard	1 tsp
½ tsp	salt	½ tsp
½ tsp	paprika, preferably Hungarian	½ tsp
½ tsp	cracked black peppercorns	½ tsp
350 g	chicken breast meat, cut crosswise into 1 cm (½ inch) wide strips	12 oz
350 g	chicken thigh meat, cut into 1 cm (½ inch) wide strips	12 oz
1	lemon, juice only	1
15 g	unsalted butter	½ oz
1	large onion, sliced	1
5	sticks celery, cut lengthwise into 5 mm (¼ inch) strips, each strip cut into 2.5 cm (1 inch) lengths	5
1½ tbsp	flour	1½ tbsp
1.25 kg	ripe tomatoes, skinned, seeded and chopped, or 800 g (28 oz) canned tomatoes, drained and chopped	2½ lb
2	bay leaves	2
1 tbsp	olive oil	1 tbsp
250 g	okra, trimmed and cut into 2.5 cm (1 inch) lengths	8 oz
½ litre	unsalted chicken stock	16 fl oz
2	sweet peppers, (1 red, 1 green), seeded, deribbed and cut lengthwise into 5 mm (¼ inch) wide strips	2

Mix the garlic with the thyme, mustard, salt, paprika and pepper. Toss the chicken strips with one third of the spice mixture and the lemon juice. Set the chicken aside to marinate at room temperature.

Melt the butter in a large, heavy-bottomed pan over medium-high heat. Add the onion and the celery, and sauté them, stirring frequently, until the onions are translucent — about 8 minutes. Stir in the flour and the remaining spice mixture; continue cooking for 2 minutes more. Add the tomatoes and bay leaves. Reduce the heat and simmer for 15 minutes.

Meanwhile, heat the olive oil in a large, heavy frying pan over medium-high heat. Add the okra and sauté it, stirring frequently, until the pieces are well browned — about 5 minutes. Set the okra aside.

Add the marinated chicken strips, the stock and peppers to the tomato mixture. Simmer the stew for 20 minutes more, stirring several times.

Before serving, stir the okra into the stew and allow it to heat through.

EDITOR'S NOTE: *Rice pilaff makes an excellent foil for gumbo.*

Java Lamb Curry with Tamarind

Serves 4
Working time: about 30 minutes
Total time: about 1 hour and 30 minutes

Calories **375**
Protein **24g**
Cholesterol **55mg**
Total fat **24g**
Saturated fat **13g**
Sodium **380mg**

500 g	lean, boneless lamb (preferably leg or shoulder), cut into 2.5 cm (1 inch) cubes	1 lb
1 tbsp	ground coriander	1 tbsp
2 tsp	ground cumin	2 tsp
¼ tsp	crushed hot red pepper flakes or chili paste	¼ tsp
½ tsp	freshly ground black pepper	½ tsp
1 tbsp	flour	1 tbsp
1 tbsp	safflower oil	1 tbsp
1	large onion, chopped	1
1	sweet red pepper, seeded, deribbed and chopped	1
1 tbsp	finely chopped fresh ginger root	1 tbsp
2	garlic cloves, finely chopped	2
½ litre	unsalted brown stock	16 fl oz
75 g	tamarind pulp, steeped in 12.5 cl (4 fl oz) of boiling water for 10 minutes, liquid strained and reserved	2½ oz
6 tbsp	unsweetened coconut milk	6 tbsp
½ tsp	salt	½ tsp
⅛ tsp	ground cinnamon	⅛ tsp
⅛ tsp	ground cloves	⅛ tsp
1	lemon, rind julienned, juice reserved	1
200 g	cauliflower florets	7 oz
1	lemon (optional), sliced into thin rounds	1

Toss the lamb cubes with the coriander, cumin, red pepper flakes, black pepper and flour. Heat the oil in a large, heavy-bottomed pan over medium-high heat. Add the lamb cubes and sauté them, in several batches if necessary, until they are browned on all sides — about 8 minutes per batch. Stir in the onion, red pepper, ginger and garlic. Reduce the heat to medium; cover the pan and cook the mixture, stirring frequently to keep the onions from burning, for 8 minutes.

Add the stock, tamarind liquid, coconut milk, salt, cinnamon and cloves. Bring the mixture to a simmer, then reduce the heat so that the liquid barely trembles; cover the pan and cook the mixture for 45 minutes.

Stir in the lemon rind, lemon juice and cauliflower. Continue to simmer the curry, covered, until the cauliflower is tender — about 15 minutes. If you like, garnish the curry with the lemon slices before serving.

EDITOR'S NOTE: *Tamarind pulp — the peeled, compressed flesh of a tropical plant native to India — is available in many markets, including those specializing in Indian and Latin-American foods.*

If canned or frozen unsweetened coconut milk is not available, the coconut milk may be made at home: mix 6 tablespoons of desiccated coconut in a blender with 6 tablespoons of very hot water, then strain the liquid.

Chicken Stew with Courgettes and Tomatoes

Serves 4
Working time: about 35 minutes
Total time: about one hour

Calories **325**
Protein **32g**
Cholesterol **65mg**
Total fat **6g**
Saturated fat **1g**
Sodium **420mg**

1.25 kg	ripe tomatoes, skinned, seeded and chopped, or 800 g (28 oz) canned tomatoes, coarsely chopped, with their juice	2½ lb
35 cl	unsalted chicken stock	12 fl oz
1 tsp	sugar	1 tsp
2	garlic cloves, finely chopped	2
1 tsp	dried basil	1 tsp
½ tsp	chili powder	½ tsp
½ tsp	salt	½ tsp
	freshly ground black pepper	
2	chicken breasts, skinned	2
90 g	wide egg noodles	3 oz
250 g	courgettes, trimmed and cut into 1 cm (½ inch) thick rounds	8 oz

Put the tomatoes, stock, sugar, garlic, basil, chili powder, salt and some pepper into a large, heavy-bottomed pan over medium heat. Bring the liquid to a simmer and cook the mixture for 10 minutes.

Add the chicken breasts to the pan and poach them for 12 minutes. With a slotted spoon, remove the slightly undercooked breasts and set them aside.

Cook the noodles in 1.5 litres (2½ pints) of boiling water with ¾ teaspoon of salt for 3 minutes. Drain the noodles well, then add them to the stew along with the courgette rounds. When the chicken breasts are cool enough to handle, remove the meat from the bones. Cut the meat into 1 cm (½ inch) pieces and return it to the pan. Continue cooking the stew until the courgettes are tender — about 5 minutes more.

Tangerine Beef Stew

Serves 4
Working time: about 40 minutes
Total time: about 2 hours and 30 minutes

Calories **595**
Protein **29g**
Cholesterol **70mg**
Total fat **17g**
Saturated fat **4g**
Sodium **380mg**

3 tbsp	safflower oil	3 tbsp
500 g	stewing beef, trimmed of all fat and cut into 2.5 cm (1 inch) cubes	1 lb
½ tbsp	Chinese five-spice powder	½ tbsp
1 tbsp	flour	1 tbsp
1	garlic clove, finely chopped	1
2 tsp	finely chopped fresh ginger root	2 tsp
2	leeks, trimmed, green tops discarded, white parts split and thinly sliced	2
¼ litre	red wine	8 fl oz
½ litre	unsalted brown stock	16 fl oz
3	strips tangerine rind, each about 5 cm (2 inches) long and 2.5 cm (1 inch) wide, pinned together with 1 whole clove	3
4 tbsp	fresh tangerine juice	4 tbsp
250 g	fresh water chestnuts, peeled and sliced, or canned water chestnuts, drained, rinsed and sliced	8 oz
500 g	butternut squash or pumpkin, peeled, seeded and cut into rectangles about 4 cm (1½ inches) long, 2 cm (¾ inch) wide and 5 mm (¼ inch) thick	1 lb
½ tsp	salt	½ tsp
185 g	long-grain rice	6½ oz
2 tbsp	julienned tangerine rind (optional), blanched	2 tbsp

Pour 2 tablespoons of the oil into a heavy-bottomed pan over medium-high heat. Sprinkle the beef cubes with the five-spice powder and the flour and toss them to coat them evenly. Add as many beef cubes to the oil as will fit in a single layer without touching. Brown the meat well on one side, then turn the pieces and continue cooking them, turning as necessary, until they are browned on all sides. Use a slotted spoon to transfer the beef to a plate, then cook any remaining cubes.

Pour off any oil remaining in the pan and clean the pan. Reduce the heat to low and pour in the last tablespoon of oil. Add the garlic, ginger and leeks, and cook them, stirring often, for 5 minutes. Return the beef cubes to the pan. Add the wine, stock, and tangerine rind and juice. Cover and simmer gently for 1½ hours.

Add the water chestnuts, squash or pumpkin and salt, and continue simmering the stew until the squash is tender — about 20 minutes. While the water chestnuts and squash are cooking, cook the rice. Spoon the stew over the rice; garnish it, if you like, with the julienned rind.

EDITOR'S NOTE: *This recipe works equally well with stewing lamb or veal. A root vegetable such as carrot, sweet potato or turnip may be substituted for the squash.*

Veal Stew
with Red, Green and
Yellow Peppers

Serves 4
Working time: about 30 minutes
Total time: about 2 hours

Calories **255**
Protein **22g**
Cholesterol **70mg**
Total fat **12g**
Saturated fat **4g**
Sodium **230mg**

1 tbsp	safflower oil	1 tbsp
500 g	trimmed veal breast, cut into 2.5 cm (1 inch) chunks	1 lb
2	onions, chopped	2
2 tsp	fresh thyme, or ½ tsp dried thyme	2 tsp
4	garlic cloves, finely chopped	4
35 cl	unsalted veal or chicken stock	12 fl oz
12.5 cl	dry white wine	4 fl oz
¼ tsp	salt	¼ tsp
	freshly ground black pepper	
3	sweet peppers (1 red, 1 green, 1 yellow), seeded, deribbed and thinly sliced	3

Heat the safflower oil in a large, heavy-bottomed pan over medium-high heat. Add the veal chunks and sauté them, turning frequently, until they are lightly browned — about 5 minutes. Remove the veal from the pan and set it aside.

Add the onions and thyme to the pan and cook them until the onions are translucent — about 4 minutes. Stir in the garlic, then return the veal to the pan. Add the stock, wine, salt and some black pepper. Reduce the heat and simmer the stew, covered, until the veal is tender — about 1¼ hours. At the end of the cooking time, degrease the liquid (box, page 55).

Add the peppers and simmer the stew, covered, for a final 15 minutes. Serve immediately.

Rabbit Stew with Prunes

Serves 4
Working time: about 40 minutes
Total time: about 3 hours

Calories **355**
Protein **30g**
Cholesterol **60mg**
Total fat **14g**
Saturated fat **4g**
Sodium **230mg**

1.25 kg	rabbit, cut into serving pieces	2½ lb
¼ litre	red wine	8 fl oz
1	bouquet garni, made by tying together 2 fresh thyme sprigs, several parsley stems and 1 bay leaf (if fresh thyme is not available, tie up ½ tsp dried thyme in a piece of muslin with the other herbs)	1
1	onion, chopped	1
1	carrot, chopped	1
4	garlic cloves, chopped	4
	freshly ground black pepper	
	flour for dredging (about 4 tbsp)	
1 tbsp	safflower oil	1 tbsp
15 g	unsalted butter	½ oz
¼ tsp	salt	¼ tsp
½ litre	unsalted chicken stock	16 fl oz
175 g	stoned prunes	6 oz

Put the rabbit pieces into a large, non-reactive bowl with the wine, bouquet garni, onion, carrot, garlic and some pepper. Marinate the rabbit at room temperature for 2 hours, turning the pieces every now and then. Remove the rabbit pieces from the marinade and pat them dry with paper towels. Dredge the pieces in the flour so that they are lightly coated. Strain the marinade through a fine sieve into a bowl, reserving the vegetables and the liquid separately.

Heat the oil and butter together in a large, heavy-bottomed pan over medium-high heat. Add the rabbit pieces and sauté them, sprinkling them with the salt as they cook, until they are browned on each side — 3 to 4 minutes per side. Transfer the pieces to a plate.

Add the reserved onion, garlic and carrot to the pan. Sauté the vegetables, stirring constantly, until the onion is translucent — about 4 minutes. Pour in the strained marinade, then the stock; return the rabbit pieces to the pan. Bring the liquid to the boil, cover the pan and reduce the heat to maintain a simmer; braise the rabbit for 30 minutes.

Add the prunes and again cover the pan; continue simmering the stew until the rabbit feels tender when pierced with a fork — about 20 minutes. With a slotted spoon, transfer the rabbit and prunes to a heated dish and keep them warm. Increase the heat to medium-high and reduce the sauce until it is thick enough to coat the back of a spoon — about 5 minutes. Pour the sauce over the rabbit and prunes, and serve accompanied, if you like, by a dish of lightly buttered noodles.

EDITOR'S NOTE: *The amount of time required to stew rabbit varies widely according to age; if you are using one large rabbit, the time may have to be doubled.*

Rabbit Stew with Sherry

Serves 4
Working time: about 45 minutes
Total time: about 1 hour

Calories **520**
Protein **36g**
Cholesterol **60mg**
Total fat **15g**
Saturated fat **4g**
Sodium **365mg**

½ tsp	salt	½ tsp
1.25 kg	rabbit, cut into 8 serving pieces	2½ lb
4 tbsp	flour	4 tbsp
2 tsp	paprika, preferably Hungarian	2 tsp
1 tsp	chopped fresh thyme, or ¼ tsp dried thyme	1 tsp
⅛ tsp	freshly ground black pepper	⅛ tsp
1½ tbsp	safflower oil	1½ tbsp
1	onion, cut into chunks	1
1	garlic clove, finely chopped	1
¼ litre	dry sherry	8 fl oz
½ litre	unsalted chicken stock	16 fl oz
1	large ripe tomato, skinned, seeded and coarsely chopped	1
500 g	red potatoes, washed and sliced into 1 cm (½ inch) thick rounds	1 lb
2	small ears of sweetcorn, each cut into into 6 rounds	2
225 g	fresh broad beans, or 175 g (6 oz) frozen baby broad beans, thawed under hot running water	7½ oz

Sprinkle ¼ teaspoon of the salt over the rabbit pieces. Combine the flour, paprika, thyme and pepper in a bowl, and dredge the pieces in the mixture. Heat 1 tablespoon of the safflower oil in a shallow, heavy-bottomed pan over medium heat. Add the pieces and cook them until they are brown — about 2 minutes per side. Remove the rabbit and set it aside.

Add the remaining oil to the pan; then add the onion and cook, stirring frequently, until it is translucent — about 4 minutes. Add the garlic and continue cooking for 30 seconds. Return the rabbit pieces to the pan and pour in the sherry. Cook the mixture until the sherry is reduced by two thirds — 4 to 5 minutes. Add the stock and tomato, and bring the liquid to the boil. Reduce the heat and simmer the stew until the rabbit is tender — about 35 minutes.

Meanwhile, place the potatoes in a saucepan, cover them with cold water, and bring the water to the boil. Reduce the heat to maintain a strong simmer; cook the potatoes until they are tender — about 5 minutes.

Bring 1 litre (1¾ pints) of water to the boil in another saucepan. Add the sweetcorn and cook for 5 minutes. Remove the rounds with a slotted spoon and set them aside. If you are using fresh broad beans, blanch them in the same boiling water for 8 to 10 minutes, then drain them. (But do not blanch frozen beans.)

When the rabbit finishes cooking, add the fresh blanched or frozen broad beans and the remaining salt to the pan; reduce the heat to low and cook the stew for 2 to 3 minutes more. Divide the potatoes and sweetcorn between four individual bowls and ladle the stew over the top.

Duck Stew
with Watercress

Serves 4
Working time: about 1 hour and 30 minutes
Total time: about 3 hours

Calories **485**
Protein **30g**
Cholesterol **110mg**
Total fat **20g**
Saturated fat **7g**
Sodium **430mg**

1 tbsp	safflower oil	1 tbsp
2 kg	duck, skinned (page 55) and quartered, all visible fat removed, neck and back reserved	4 lb
½ litre	dry white wine	16 fl oz
½ litre	unsalted brown, veal or chicken stock	16 fl oz
3	onions, 1 peeled and studded with 6 cloves, the other 2 finely chopped	3
1	carrot, quartered lengthwise and cut into 2 cm (¾ inch) pieces	1
750 g	ripe tomatoes, skinned, seeded and coarsely chopped, or 400 g (14 oz) canned tomatoes, seeded and coarsely chopped	1½ lb
½ tsp	salt	½ tsp
	freshly ground black pepper	
15 g	unsalted butter	½ oz
4	garlic cloves, chopped	4
1½ tsp	fresh rosemary, or ½ tsp dried rosemary	1½ tsp
3 tbsp	flour	3 tbsp
1	bunch watercress, stemmed	1

Heat the oil in a large, heavy frying pan over medium-high heat. Add the duck quarters, neck and back, and sauté them until they are well browned on one side —

about 8 minutes. Turn the pieces over and sauté them on the second side for about 7 minutes. Then transfer the duck pieces to a large, heavy-bottomed saucepan.

Pour off and discard the fat in the frying pan. Add the wine to the frying pan and bring it to the boil, using a wooden spoon to scrape up the caramelized bits from the bottom. Boil the wine until it is reduced to about ¼ litre (8 fl oz) — 5 to 10 minutes.

Add the reduced wine to the duck along with the stock, 1 litre (1¾ pints) of water and the clove-studded onion. Slowly bring the stew to the boil over medium heat. Skim off any impurities that rise to the surface; pour in 12.5 cl (4 fl oz) of cold water and skim again. Bring the stew to the boil again, reduce the heat to maintain a simmer and skim once more. Simmer the stew for 35 minutes, turning the duck pieces once.

Add the carrot, tomatoes, ¼ teaspoon of the salt and some pepper. Simmer the stew until the duck pieces are tender — about 30 minutes more. Remove the duck pieces from the pan and set them aside; discard the neck and back. Reduce the stew liquid over high heat to about ¾ litre (1¼ pints) — 5 to 10 minutes.

While the stew liquid is reducing, melt the butter in a saucepan over medium heat. Add the finely chopped onions, garlic, rosemary and the remaining salt; cook, stirring from time to time, for 10 minutes. Add 12.5 cl (4 fl oz) of the reduced stew liquid to the pan and continue cooking until the onions are very limp — about 10 minutes more.

Stir the flour into the pan, then whisk in another ¼ litre (8 fl oz) of the reduced stew liquid. Simmer the mixture for 1 minute, then transfer it to a blender or food processor and purée it, stopping once to scrape down the sides. Whisk the purée into the stew liquid.

With a sharp knife, remove the duck meat from the bones. Discard the bones and cut the meat into 1 cm (½ inch) pieces. Add the duck pieces to the stew liquid. Grind in some more pepper. Reheat the mixture over low heat for 5 minutes, then stir in the watercress and immediately remove the pan from the heat. Serve the stew with egg noodles.

Lamb-Spinach Stew with Orzo

Serves 4
Working time: about 15 minutes
Total time: about 1 hour and 15 minutes

Calories **485**
Protein **29g**
Cholesterol **55mg**
Total fat **19g**
Saturated fat **9g**
Sodium **425mg**

1 tbsp	safflower oil	1 tbsp
1	onion, chopped	1
6	garlic cloves, finely chopped	6
1 tsp	ground cumin	1 tsp
1 tsp	ground coriander	1 tsp
500 g	boneless lamb, cut into 2.5 cm (1 inch) chunks	1 lb
½ tsp	salt	½ tsp
	freshly ground black pepper	
¾ litre	unsalted brown stock	1¼ pints
210 g	orzo (rice-shaped pasta)	7 oz
500 g	spinach, washed and stemmed	1 lb
½	lime, juice only	½

Heat the oil in a large, heavy-bottomed pan over medium-high heat. Add the onion, garlic, cumin and coriander, and sauté the mixture until the onion is translucent — about 4 minutes. Add the lamb and cook it until it loses all traces of redness — about 3 minutes. Add the salt and a generous grinding of pepper. Then pour in the stock, reduce the heat, and simmer the liquid, covered, until the lamb is tender — about 1 hour.

In a large saucepan, about 15 minutes before the lamb is done, add the orzo to 3 litres (5 pints) of boiling water with 1½ teaspoons of salt. Start testing the orzo after 10 minutes and cook it until it is al dente. Drain the orzo and rinse it under cold running water.

When the lamb is done, degrease the liquid (box, page 55). Then add the spinach to the pan and tightly cover it. Cook the spinach until it is wilted — about 3 minutes. Stir in the cooked orzo and the lime juice just before serving the stew.

Veal Stew with Pearl Onions and Grainy Mustard

Serves 6
Working time: about 15 minutes
Total time: about 1 hour

Calories **270**
Protein **23g**
Cholesterol **80mg**
Total fat **13g**
Saturated fat **7g**
Sodium **135mg**

750 g	stewing veal, trimmed and cut into 2.5 cm (1 inch) cubes	1½ lb
½ litre	unsalted veal or chicken stock	16 fl oz
12.5 cl	dry white wine	4 fl oz
2	small onions, each stuck with 2 cloves	2
1 tsp	fresh thyme, or ¼ tsp dried thyme	1 tsp
25 g	unsalted butter	¾ oz
4 tbsp	flour	4 tbsp
1	large carrot, cut diagonally into 5 mm (¼ inch) thick slices	1
250 g	pearl onions, peeled	8 oz
1 tbsp	grainy mustard	1 tbsp
4 tbsp	single cream	4 tbsp
⅛ tsp	white pepper	⅛ tsp

Combine the veal, stock, wine, the clove-studded onions and ½ litre (16 fl oz) of water in a large pan. Bring the liquid to the boil and skim off any impurities that rise to the surface. Add the thyme, then reduce the heat. Simmer the meat, partially covered, until it is just tender — about 40 minutes. Discard the onions.

Melt the butter in a small pan over medium heat. Whisk in the flour and cook, whisking constantly, for 3 minutes. Continuing to whisk, slowly pour in ½ litre (16 fl oz) of the veal-cooking liquid until a smooth mixture results. Transfer this liquid to the other pan and bring the stew to the boil. Reduce the heat, add the carrot and pearl onions, and stir in the mustard. Simmer until the vegetables are tender — about 10 minutes. Gently stir in the cream and pepper; serve immediately.

Mexican Chicken Stew with Chilies

THIS STEW IS BEST SERVED OVER RICE.

Serves 4
Working time: about 25 minutes
Total time: about 45 minutes

Calories **260**
Protein **30g**
Cholesterol **75mg**
Total fat **11g**
Saturated fat **2g**
Sodium **680mg**

1 litre	unsalted chicken stock	1¾ pints
2	large dried mild chili peppers, stemmed, seeded, rinsed and quartered	2
500 g	boneless chicken breasts, skinned and cut into 2.5 cm (1 inch) cubes	1 lb
1 tsp	salt	1 tsp
¼ tsp	freshly ground black pepper	¼ tsp
1½ tbsp	corn or safflower oil	1½ tbsp
1 tbsp	finely chopped garlic	1 tbsp
½ tsp	ground cumin	½ tsp
⅛ tsp	ground cloves	⅛ tsp
350 g	chayote squash or young courgettes, cut into 1 cm (½ inch) chunks	12 oz
1	onion, coarsely chopped	1
2 tsp	cornflour, mixed with 2 tbsp water	2 tsp
45 g	fresh coriander, chopped	1½ oz

Bring ¼ litre (8 fl oz) of the stock to the boil in a small saucepan. Add the chilies, then reduce the heat, cover the pan, and simmer the liquid for 5 minutes. Turn off the heat and let the mixture stand for 5 minutes. Purée the chilies in a blender or food processor with 4 tablespoons of the liquid. Blend in the remaining liquid and then set the purée aside.

Toss the chicken cubes with the salt and pepper. Heat 1 tablespoon of the corn or safflower oil in a large, heavy-bottomed sauté pan over medium-high heat. Add the chicken cubes and sauté them, stirring frequently, until the cubes are browned — about 2 minutes. Remove the cubes and set them aside.

Reduce the heat under the sauté pan to low; add the remaining oil, the garlic, cumin and cloves. Cook, stirring constantly, until the garlic has softened —about 3 minutes. Add the chili purée and the remaining stock.

Bring the liquid to the boil, then add the squash or courgettes and onion. Reduce the heat, cover the pan and simmer the mixture for 10 minutes. Remove the lid and increase the heat to medium; add the reserved chicken cubes, then stir in the cornflour mixture. Simmer the stew until it thickens slightly and is shiny — 3 to 4 minutes. Stir in the coriander just before serving.

Pork and Apple Stew

Serves 4
Working time: about 30 minutes
Total time: about 1 hour and 45 minutes

Calories **280**
Protein **24g**
Cholesterol **70mg**
Total fat **12g**
Saturated fat **2g**
Sodium **265mg**

2 tbsp	safflower oil	2 tbsp
500 g	boneless pork shoulder, fat trimmed away, cut into 2.5 cm (1 inch) chunks	1 lb
1	onion, sliced	1
3	cooking apples, 2 cut into large chunks, 1 cored and thinly sliced	3
1 tsp	dried sage	1 tsp
¼ tsp	salt	¼ tsp
	freshly ground black pepper	
¾ litre	unsalted brown stock	1¼ pints
1	ripe tomato, skinned, seeded and chopped	1

Heat 1 tablespoon of the oil in a heavy-bottomed pan over medium-high heat. Add the pork and onion, and sauté them until the pork is lightly browned and the onion is translucent — about 5 minutes. Add the apple chunks, sage, salt, a generous grinding of pepper and the stock. Reduce the heat to maintain a simmer, then cover the pan and cook the stew until the pork is tender — about 1 hour.

Remove the pork from the pan and set it aside. Carefully skim as much fat from the surface of the liquid as you can. Purée the apple chunks and onion with their cooking liquid in several batches in a food mill. (Alternatively, purée the mixture in a food processor, then press the purée through a fine sieve with a wooden spoon.) Return the purée and the pork to the pan, and heat the stew over medium-high heat.

While the stew is heating, pour the remaining safflower oil into a heavy frying pan over medium-high heat. Add the uncooked apple slices and sauté them until they are lightly browned. Stir the apple slices and the tomato into the hot stew and serve at once.

EDITOR'S NOTE: *This stew may be prepared up to 24 hours in advance, but the apple slices must be sautéed and added just before serving.*

Oxtails Braised with Carrots

Serves 4
Working time: about 35 minutes
Total time: about 3 hours

Calories **295**
Protein **32g**
Cholesterol **75mg**
Total fat **9g**
Saturated fat **3g**
Sodium **245mg**

1 tbsp	safflower oil	1 tbsp
1	bunch spring onions, trimmed and chopped	1
1½ tbsp	finely chopped fresh ginger root	1½ tbsp
2	garlic cloves, finely chopped	2
½ litre	unsalted brown stock	16 fl oz
¼ litre	dry sherry	8 fl oz
2 tsp	fermented black beans, crushed	2 tsp
1 tsp	chili sauce	1 tsp
2 tsp	hoisin sauce	2 tsp
1.5 kg	oxtails, trimmed of all fat and blanched in boiling water for 3 minutes	3 lb
5	carrots, roll-cut (box, page 112)	5
175 g	fresh Asian wheat noodles	6 oz

In a heavy pan large enough to hold the oxtails in a single layer, heat the oil over medium-high heat. Add the spring onions, ginger and garlic, and sauté them for 2 minutes. Pour in the stock, ½ litre (16 fl oz) of water and the sherry, then stir in the crushed black beans, chili sauce and hoisin sauce. Add the oxtails. Bring the liquid to the boil, then reduce the heat to very low and cook the oxtails, covered, for 1 hour. Turn the oxtails over and cook them until they are very tender — about 1½ hours more.

Add the carrots and simmer them until they are just tender — 15 to 20 minutes.

Pour the stew into a colander set over a large bowl. Remove the oxtail meat from the bones and return it to the pan along with the carrots and other solids. Degrease the liquid *(box, page 55)*, then pour it back into the pan. Reheat the stew over medium heat.

Add the noodles to 2 litres (3½ pints) of boiling ▶

water with 1 teaspoon of salt. Start testing the noodles after 3 minutes and cook them until they are *al dente*. Drain the noodles, then divide them between six soup bowls. Top the noodles with the oxtails and carrots, ladle some liquid over all and serve immediately.

A Cut above the Rest

ROLL-CUTTING A CARROT. Peel a carrot or other cylindrical vegetable. With a chef's knife, cut off the tip at an oblique angle. Roll the vegetable a quarter or third of a turn; holding the knife at the same angle, cut off another piece — it will have non-parallel ends. Continue until you reach the stem end.

Sauerbraten Stew
with Crystallized Ginger

Serves 4
Working time: about 30 minutes
Total time: about 3 hours (includes marinating)

Calories **345**
Protein **27g**
Cholesterol **75mg**
Total fat **10g**
Saturated fat **3g**
Sodium **390mg**

1 tbsp	safflower oil	1 tbsp
500 g	lean stewing beef, trimmed of fat, sliced 5 mm (¼ inch) thick and cut into 2.5 cm (1 inch) squares	1 lb
4 tbsp	crystallized ginger, cut into thin strips	4 tbsp
1	onion, finely chopped	1
1	carrot, finely chopped	1
1	stick celery, finely chopped	1
1	bay leaf	1
5	juniper berries, or 1 tbsp gin	5
¾ tsp	ground allspice	¾ tsp
½ tsp	salt	½ tsp
	freshly ground black pepper	
½ litre	red wine	16 fl oz
1 tbsp	red wine vinegar	1 tbsp
¼ litre	unsalted brown stock	8 fl oz
1	slice wholemeal bread, crumbled	1
2 tsp	flour	2 tsp

Heat the oil in a large, heavy frying pan over medium-high heat. Add the beef squares and crystallized ginger, and cook them, turning the meat occasionally, until the beef is well browned — about 10 minutes. Transfer the beef and ginger to a large, non-reactive saucepan or fireproof casserole.

Reduce the heat under the frying pan to medium, then add the onion, carrot, celery, bay leaf, juniper berries or gin, allspice, salt and some pepper. Cook the mixture, stirring and scraping with a wooden spoon to loosen any bits of beef, for 5 minutes. Pour in the wine and vinegar, and simmer the mixture for 1 minute. Transfer the vegetable mixture to the saucepan. Stir to combine the ingredients, then cover the pan and let the stew stand for 1 hour off the heat to marinate the beef and vegetables in the liquid. Remove the bay leaf.

Pour the stock and 17.5 cl (6 fl oz) of water into the pan. Partially cover the pan and slowly bring the liquid to a simmer. Simmer the stew, stirring occasionally, for 40 minutes. Mix the crumbled bread with the flour and stir them into the stew. Continue cooking the stew until the beef is tender — about 40 minutes more.

Beef Stew with Stout

Serves 6
Working time: about 40 minutes
Total time: about 2 hours and 15 minutes

Calories **260**
Protein **27g**
Cholesterol **75mg**
Total fat **10g**
Saturated fat **3g**
Sodium **265mg**

1½ tbsp	safflower oil	1½ tbsp
750 g	lean stewing beef, trimmed and cut into 2.5 cm (1 inch) cubes	1½ lb
1	large onion, chopped	1
250 g	button mushrooms, wiped clean, halved	8 oz
2 tbsp	dark brown sugar	2 tbsp
½ litre	unsalted brown or veal stock	16 fl oz
35 cl	stout or dark beer	12 fl oz
½ tsp	salt	½ tsp
	freshly ground black pepper	

Heat 1 tablespoon of the safflower oil in a large, heavy frying pan over medium-high heat. Add the beef cubes and sauté them, turning them frequently, until they are browned all over — about 8 minutes. Using a slotted spoon, transfer the beef to a heavy-bottomed saucepan.

Add the remaining oil to the frying pan along with the onion, mushrooms and brown sugar. Sauté the mixture, stirring frequently, until the mushrooms begin to brown and their liquid has evaporated — about 10 minutes. Transfer the onion-mushroom mixture to the saucepan, then add the stock, the stout or dark beer, the salt and some pepper.

Reduce the heat to very low, cover the saucepan, and gently simmer the stew until the beef is tender — 1½ to 2 hours.

Chicken Stew in Whole Green and Red Peppers

Serves 4
Working time: about 25 minutes
Total time: about 50 minutes

Calories **200**
Protein **16g**
Cholesterol **45mg**
Total fat **11g**
Saturated fat **2g**
Sodium **330mg**

1½ tbsp	virgin olive oil	1½ tbsp
2	large garlic cloves, finely chopped	2
1	onion, cut in half, the halves cut into pieces about 2.5 cm (1 inch) square	1
4	chicken thighs, skinned and boned, the meat cut into 2.5 cm (1 inch) chunks	4
1 tbsp	dried oregano	1 tbsp
	freshly ground black pepper	
½ tsp	salt	½ tsp
750 g	ripe tomatoes, skinned, seeded and coarsely chopped, with their juice, or 400 g (14 oz) canned whole tomatoes, with their juice	1½ lb
3	sweet green peppers, 1 seeded, deribbed and cut into 2.5 cm (1 inch) squares	3
3	sweet red peppers, 1 seeded, deribbed and cut into 2.5 cm (1 inch) squares	3

Pour the oil into a large, heavy-bottomed saucepan or sauté pan over medium-high heat. When the oil is hot, add the garlic and onion and sauté them, stirring often, for 2 minutes. Add the chicken, oregano, pepper and salt, and sauté the chicken until the pieces are golden-brown — about 5 minutes.

Reduce the heat and add the tomatoes with their juice to the pan; if you are using canned whole tomatoes, coarsely chop the tomatoes in the pan. Then add the squares of green and red pepper. Cover the pan and simmer the stew until the chicken is tender and the peppers are soft — about 20 minutes. If the stew absorbs all the liquid, pour in 12.5 cl (4 fl oz) of water.

While the stew is simmering, carefully cut the top off each of the remaining peppers. Seed and derib the peppers. If necessary, shave a thin slice from the bottom of each pepper so it will stand upright. Set a steamer in a saucepan and pour in enough water to barely reach the bottom of the steamer. Bring the water to the boil, put the peppers, including lids, in the steamer and tightly cover the pan. Steam the peppers until they are tender — 5 to 10 minutes.

Stand each steamed pepper in a small bowl. Spoon the stew into the peppers; distribute any remaining stew around the peppers, and serve immediately.

Beef Stew with Apricots and Couscous

Serves 4
Working time: about 10 minutes
Total time: about 1 hour and 15 minutes

Calories **475**
Protein **34g**
Cholesterol **75mg**
Total fat **10g**
Saturated fat **3g**
Sodium **450mg**

½ tsp	salt	½ tsp
	freshly ground black pepper	
500 g	lean stewing beef, cut into 2.5 cm (1 inch) cubes	1 lb
2 tbsp	plain flour	2 tbsp
1 tbsp	safflower oil	1 tbsp
1	small onion, thinly sliced	1
1	garlic clove, finely chopped	1
12.5 cl	dry vermouth	4 fl oz
½ tsp	ground cinnamon	½ tsp
175 g	dried apricots, cut in half if large	6 oz
¾ litre	unsalted brown stock	1¼ pints
500 g	peas, shelled, or 145 g (5 oz) frozen peas, thawed	1 lb
175 g	couscous	6 oz

Sprinkle ¼ teaspoon of the salt and some pepper over the beef cubes, then dredge them in the flour.

Heat the oil in a large, non-reactive, fireproof casserole over medium-high heat. Add the beef cubes and sauté them, turning them frequently, until they are browned on all sides — about 3 minutes. Push the beef to one side of the pan; reduce the heat to medium, add the onion and garlic, and cook them, stirring often, until the onion is translucent — about 4 minutes. Stir in the vermouth and cinnamon. Scrape the bottom of the pan with a wooden spoon to dissolve the caramelized juices and bits of flour. Simmer the liquid until it thickens — 2 to 3 minutes.

Stir in one third of the apricots and half of the stock. Bring the liquid to a gentle simmer over medium-low heat and cook it, covered, for 30 minutes. Stir in the remaining stock and cook the mixture, covered, for 20 minutes more. Add the remaining apricots along with the fresh peas, if you are using them (do not add the frozen peas yet). Cook the stew for an additional 10 minutes; if you are using frozen peas, stir them in about 3 minutes before the end of the cooking time.

To prepare the couscous, bring 35 cl (12 fl oz) of water to the boil in a small saucepan with the remaining salt. Remove the pan from the heat, stir in the couscous and let it stand, covered, for 5 minutes. Fluff the couscous with a fork and serve it blanketed with the stew.

Seafood Stew with Water Chestnuts

Serves 4
Working time: about 35 minutes
Total time: about 50 minutes

Calories **240**		
Protein **25g**		
Cholesterol **100mg**		
Total fat **6g**		
Saturated fat **1g**		
Sodium **165mg**		

350 g	bass or cod fillet	12 oz
1½ tbsp	finely chopped fresh ginger root	1½ tbsp
1	garlic clove, finely chopped	1
4 tbsp	mirin (sweet Japanese rice wine) or sweet sherry	4 tbsp
¼ tsp	freshly ground black pepper	¼ tsp
250 g	large fresh prawns, peeled, deveined if necessary	8 oz
1 tbsp	peanut oil	1 tbsp
¼ litre	fish stock	8 fl oz
1 tsp	dark soy sauce	1 tsp
2	carrots, thinly sliced diagonally	2
4	spring onions, trimmed and thinly sliced diagonally	4
8	fresh water chestnuts, peeled and thinly sliced, or canned water chestnuts, drained, rinsed and thinly sliced	8
125 g	mushrooms, wiped clean, thinly sliced	4 oz
4 tsp	cornflour, mixed with 2 tbsp water	4 tsp
1	bunch watercress, stemmed	1

Rinse the fish under cold running water, then pat it dry with paper towels and slice it into 2.5 cm (1 inch) cubes.

In a bowl, combine the ginger, garlic, mirin or sherry, and pepper. Add the fish and prawns, stir to coat them with the marinade, and let the mixture stand at room temperature for 20 minutes.

Drain and reserve the marinade. Heat the oil in a large fireproof casserole over medium-high heat. Add the fish and prawns, and stir-fry them until they are opaque — 2 to 3 minutes. Remove the seafood from the casserole and set it aside while you finish the dish.

Pour the stock, soy sauce and reserved marinade into the casserole. Add the carrots, spring onions, water chestnuts and mushrooms. Bring the stew to the boil, then reduce the heat to maintain a gentle simmer, and cover the casserole. Cook the stew until the carrots are tender — about 8 minutes.

Stir in the cornflour mixture, watercress and reserved seafood. Return the stew to the boil and cook it for 2 minutes more to thicken it. Serve immediately.

Southwest Gumbo

Serves 8
Working time: about 40 minutes
Total time: about 1 hour

Calories **290**
Protein **32g**
Cholesterol **110mg**
Total fat **8g**
Saturated fat **1g**
Sodium **390mg**

3 tbsp	olive oil	3 tbsp
250 g	fresh okra, trimmed and cut into 2.5 cm (1 inch) lengths	8 oz
1	large onion, coarsely chopped	1
120 g	celery, very finely chopped	4 oz
1	large garlic clove, finely chopped	1
1	large shallot, finely chopped	1
3 tbsp	masa harina	3 tbsp
1 tsp	filé powder (optional)	1 tsp
1 tsp	salt	1 tsp
1 tsp	sugar	1 tsp
1 tsp	freshly ground black pepper	1 tsp
1 tsp	ground cumin	1 tsp
1 litre	fish stock	1¾ pints
1	sweet green pepper, seeded, deribbed and coarsely chopped	1
1	sweet red pepper, seeded, deribbed and coarsely chopped	1
500 g	green tomatoes, cut into thin wedges	1 lb
6 tbsp	chopped fresh parsley	6 tbsp
2 tbsp	finely chopped fresh coriander	2 tbsp
8	drops Tabasco sauce	8
500 g	halibut steaks, rinsed, skinned and cut into 2.5 cm (1 inch) cubes	1 lb
500 g	monkfish fillet, rinsed and cut into 2.5 cm (1 inch) pieces	1 lb
500 g	prawns, peeled, deveined if necessary	1 lb

Heat 1 tablespoon of the olive oil in a large, heavy, non-reactive pan over medium-high heat. Add the okra and sauté it, turning frequently, until it is evenly browned — about 5 minutes. Remove the okra and set it aside.

Reduce the heat to medium and pour the remaining oil into the pan. Add the onion and celery and cook them, covered, until the onion is translucent — about 5 minutes. Add the garlic and shallot and cook the mixture, stirring constantly, for 2 minutes more. Sprinkle in the masa harina, filé powder if using, salt, sugar, black pepper and cumin. Whisk in the stock and bring the liquid to the boil. Add the okra, the green pepper and red pepper, and the green tomatoes. Partially cover the pan, then reduce the heat to maintain a simmer and cook the gumbo, stirring occasionally, for 8 to 10 minutes.

Stir in the parsley, coriander and Tabasco sauce. Add the halibut, monkfish and prawns, and gently stir the gumbo to incorporate the fish and prawns. Cover the pan, reduce the heat to low and cook the gumbo for 5 minutes more. Serve immediately.

EDITOR'S NOTE: *Masa harina — finely ground white or yellow hominy (processed dried maize kernels) — may be obtained at speciality food shops. If it is unavailable, substitute plain flour. Filé powder, used to flavour and thicken Creole soups and stews, is made from dried young sassafras leaves.*

Cod Stewed with Onions, Potatoes, Sweetcorn and Tomatoes

Serves 6
Working time: about 15 minutes
Total time: about 1 hour

Calories **310**
Protein **19g**
Cholesterol **30mg**
Total fat **4g**
Saturated fat **1g**
Sodium **305mg**

1 tbsp	virgin olive oil	1 tbsp
500 g	onions, thinly sliced	1 lb
1 kg	waxy potatoes, peeled and thinly sliced	2 lb
500 g	fresh or frozen sweetcorn kernels	1 lb
½	green pepper, seeded, deribbed and diced	½
	Tabasco sauce	
500 g	cod (or haddock), skinned, rinsed under cold running water, and cut into chunks	1 lb
1.25 kg	ripe tomatoes, skinned, seeded and chopped, or 800 g (28 oz) canned whole tomatoes, drained and chopped	2½ lb
¼ tsp	salt	¼ tsp
	freshly ground black pepper	
	fresh coriander leaves for garnish (optional)	

In a large, heavy-bottomed pan, heat the oil over medium heat. Add a layer of onions and a layer of potatoes. Sprinkle some of the sweetcorn and green pepper on top. Dribble a few drops of Tabasco sauce over the vegetables. Add a layer of fish and tomatoes and season with a little of the salt and some pepper. Repeat the process, building up successive layers, until the remaining vegetables and fish are used. Cover the pan and cook over medium-low heat until the potatoes are done — about 45 minutes. Garnish the stew with the coriander leaves if you are using them. Serve at once.

Mediterranean Fish Chowder

Serves 6
Working time: about 40 minutes
Total time: about 1 hour and 30 minutes

Calories **235**
Protein **23g**
Cholesterol **120mg**
Total fat **3g**
Saturated fat **1g**
Sodium **315mg**

250 g	fresh prawns, peeled, deveined if necessary, shells reserved	8 oz
2	leeks, trimmed, split and washed thoroughly to remove all grit, green and white parts sliced separately	2
12	black peppercorns	12
1 tsp	chopped fresh thyme, or ¼ tsp dried thyme	1 tsp
1 tsp	chopped fresh rosemary, or ¼ tsp dried rosemary	1 tsp
1	bay leaf	1
1 kg	mussels, scrubbed and debearded	2 lb
250 g	white crab meat, picked over	8 oz
1	garlic clove, finely chopped	1
	pinch of saffron	
4 tbsp	dry white wine	4 tbsp
500 g	waxy potatoes, peeled and cut into 2.5 cm (1 inch) chunks	1 lb
750 g	ripe tomatoes, skinned, seeded and chopped, or 400 g (14 oz) canned tomatoes, drained and crushed	1½ lb

Pour 1 litre (1¾ pints) of water into a large pan. Add the prawn shells, green leek parts, peppercorns, thyme, rosemary and bay leaf. Bring the broth to the boil, then reduce the heat and simmer the liquid for 15 minutes. Add the mussels to the broth and cook them until they open — about 3 minutes. Transfer the opened mussels to a bowl. Cook the remaining mussels for 2 minutes more and transfer the opened ones to the bowl; discard any that remain closed.

Working over the bowl to catch their juices, free the mussels from their shells and drop them into the bowl. Add the prawns, crab meat, garlic, saffron and wine, and stir well. Let the shellfish marinate at room temperature for 30 minutes.

In the meantime, strain the broth through a fine sieve, discarding the solids. Return the broth to the pan over medium-high heat. Add the white leek parts and the potatoes, and cook them until the leeks are tender — about 15 minutes. Stir in the tomatoes and cook the stew until the potatoes are tender — about 5 minutes more.

Add the shellfish and its marinade to the stew. Cook the stew until the prawns are opaque and the other shellfish are warmed through — about 3 minutes. Serve immediately.

Smoked and Fresh Salmon in Red Wine Stew

Serves 8
Working time: about 45 minutes
Total time: about 1 hour and 15 minutes

Calories **240**
Protein **15g**
Cholesterol **20mg**
Total fat **7g**
Saturated fat **1g**
Sodium **90mg**

2	red potatoes, scrubbed and cut into 1 cm (½ inch) chunks	2
1 tbsp	safflower oil	1 tbsp
250 g	mushrooms, wiped clean and sliced	8 oz
300 g	pearl onions, blanched in boiling water for 30 seconds and peeled	10 oz
½ tsp	sugar	½ tsp
¾ litre	fish stock or unsalted chicken stock	1¼ pints
¾ litre	red wine	1¼ pints
½ tsp	fresh thyme, or ⅛ tsp dried thyme	½ tsp
1	bay leaf	1
1 tbsp	cornflour, mixed with 2 tbsp water	1 tbsp
60 g	smoked salmon, cut into 5 mm (¼ inch) squares	2 oz
500 g	salmon fillet, skinned, rinsed and cut into 2.5 cm (1 inch) square pieces	1 lb

Put the potato cubes into a saucepan and pour in enough water to cover them by about 5 cm (2 inches). Bring the water to the boil, then reduce the heat and simmer the potatoes until they are tender — about 10 minutes. Drain the potatoes and set them aside.

While the potatoes are cooking, heat the oil in a large, non-reactive heavy-bottomed pan over medium-high heat. Add the mushrooms and cook them, stirring frequently, until they are browned and the liquid has evaporated — about 5 minutes. Remove the mushrooms from the pan and set them aside.

Add the onions, sugar and ¼ litre (8 fl oz) of the stock to the pan. Cook, stirring frequently and scraping the bottom of the pan, until almost all the liquid has evaporated and the onions begin to caramelize — about 10 minutes. Then remove the onions and set them aside with the mushrooms.

Pour the wine and the remaining stock into the pan. Add the thyme and bay leaf. Bring the liquid to the boil, stirring constantly and scraping the bottom of the pan to dissolve the caramelized juices. Lower the heat, then partially cover the pan and simmer the liquid until it is reduced to approximately 1 litre (1¾ pints) — about 30 minutes.

Add the potatoes, mushrooms, onions and the cornflour mixture to the liquid and bring it to the boil. Reduce the heat, stir in the smoked salmon and fresh salmon, and simmer the stew until the salmon is opaque — 2 to 3 minutes. Serve hot.

Squid and Red Bean Stew

KIDNEY BEANS CONTAIN TOXINS CALLED LECTINS. TO DESTROY
THE LECTINS, BE SURE TO BOIL THE BEANS FOR 10 MINUTES
BEFORE ADDING THEM TO THE DISH.

Serves 6
Working time: about 1 hour and 45 minutes
Total time: about 9 hours and 45 minutes (includes soaking)

Calories **275**
Protein **23g**
Cholesterol **210mg**
Total fat **4g**
Saturated fat **0g**
Sodium **265mg**

185 g	dried red kidney beans, picked over, soaked for 8 hours (or overnight) in cold water, then drained	6½ oz
1 tbsp	safflower oil	1 tbsp
1	small onion, thinly sliced	1
1	garlic clove, finely chopped	1
12.5 cl	Marsala	4 fl oz
250 g	mushrooms, wiped clean, large ones quartered, smaller ones halved	8 oz
750 g	ripe tomatoes, skinned, seeded and finely chopped, or 400 g (14 oz) canned tomatoes, chopped, with their juice	1½ lb
350 g	squid, cleaned	12 oz
175 g	green beans, trimmed and cut into 5 cm (2 inch) lengths	6 oz
1 tsp	fresh oregano, or ¼ tsp dried oregano	1 tsp
½ tsp	salt	½ tsp
	freshly ground black pepper	

Cook the kidney beans in ¾ litre (1¼ pints) of boiling water for 10 minutes, then drain and set aside.

Pour the oil into a large pan over medium heat. Add the sliced onion and cook it, stirring often, until it is translucent — about 4 minutes. Add the chopped garlic and cook it, stirring, for 1 minute. Pour in the Marsala and continue cooking until the liquid is reduced by half — 3 to 4 minutes.

Stir in the mushrooms, tomatoes, drained beans and 1.25 litres (2 pints) of water. Increase the heat to high and bring the liquid to the boil. Immediately reduce the heat to maintain a simmer; cook the mixture, covered, for about 20 minutes.

While the liquid is simmering, prepare the squid. Cut the squid into strips about 5 cm (2 inches) long and 5 mm (¼ inch) wide. Cut the tentacles into 5 cm (2 inch) lengths. Add the squid to the stew and continue simmering the stew until the beans are tender — about 1 hour more.

While the stew is cooking, bring 1 litre (1¾ pints) of water to the boil in a saucepan. Add the green beans and cook them until they are barely tender — about 8 minutes. Drain the green beans and set them aside.

When the beans in the stew are tender, add the green beans to the pan with the oregano, salt and some pepper. Simmer the stew over low heat until the green beans are heated through — 3 to 4 minutes. Serve the stew piping hot.

Caribbean Fish Stew

Serves 4
Working time: about 15 minutes
Total time: about 45 minutes

Calories **265**
Protein **25g**
Cholesterol **45mg**
Total fat **5g**
Saturated fat **1g**
Sodium **250mg**

500 g	red snapper or redfish fillets, skin left on	1 lb
4 tbsp	dry white wine	4 tbsp
2 tbsp	dark rum	2 tbsp
1 tbsp	finely chopped fresh ginger root	1 tbsp
1	garlic clove, finely chopped	1
	freshly ground black pepper	
1 tbsp	safflower oil	1 tbsp
1	onion, cut into small chunks	1
2 tbsp	flour	2 tbsp
2 tsp	tomato paste	2 tsp
1	sweet green pepper, seeded, deribbed and cut into 2 cm (¾ inch) pieces	1
½ litre	fish stock	16 fl oz
2	ripe tomatoes, skinned, seeded and coarsely chopped	2
1	ripe mango, peeled and cut into 2 cm (¾ inch) pieces	1
¼ tsp	salt	¼ tsp

Rinse the fillets under cold running water and pat them dry with paper towels. Cut the fillets into 4 cm (1½ inch) squares and set them aside.

In a bowl, combine the wine, rum, ginger, garlic and some pepper. Marinate the fish pieces in this mixture for 30 minutes in the refrigerator.

When the fish has marinated for 20 minutes, pour the oil into a non-reactive, heavy-bottomed pan over medium heat. Add the onion chunks and cook them, stirring occasionally, until they begin to brown — 6 to 8 minutes. Stir in the flour, then the tomato paste and the green pepper. Slowly whisk in the stock. Drain the marinade from the fish and add it to the pan. Bring the liquid to a simmer and cook it for 3 minutes.

Add the fish, tomatoes, mango and salt to the pan. Cover, and simmer until the fish is opaque and flakes easily — about 7 minutes. Serve immediately.

Prawn Creole

Serves 4
Working time: about 35 minutes
Total time: about 1 hour and 15 minutes

Calories **325**
Protein **23g**
Cholesterol **165mg**
Total fat **6g**
Saturated fat **1g**
Sodium **240mg**

4 tsp	safflower oil	4 tsp
1	large onion, thinly sliced	1
2	garlic cloves, finely chopped	2
1 tbsp	flour	1 tbsp
1 tbsp	chili powder	1 tbsp
600 g	large uncooked prawns, peeled, deveined if necessary, shells reserved	1¼ lb
¼ litre	dry white vermouth	8 fl oz
90 g	long-grain rice	3 oz
3	small sweet green peppers, seeded, deribbed and cut lengthwise into thin strips	3
1	stick celery, thinly sliced on the diagonal	1
750 g	ripe tomatoes, skinned, seeded and coarsely chopped, with their juice, or 400 g (14 oz) canned tomatoes, chopped, with their juice	1½ lb
¼ tsp	filé powder (optional)	¼ tsp
¼ tsp	salt	¼ tsp
30 g	lean ham (optional), julienned	1 oz

Heat 2 teaspoons of the oil in a heavy-bottomed saucepan over medium heat. Add the onion slices and cook them, stirring frequently, until they are browned — 8 to 10 minutes. Remove half of the slices and set them aside.

Add the garlic and cook it for 1 minute. Stir in the flour and chili powder, then the prawn shells, vermouth and ¼ litre (8 fl oz) of water. Bring the liquid to a simmer; reduce the heat to medium low, cover the pan and cook the mixture for 20 minutes to make a flavourful base for the stew.

Meanwhile, bring ¼ litre (8 fl oz) of water to the boil in a small saucepan. Add the rice, stir once and reduce the heat to maintain a simmer; cook the rice, covered, until the liquid is absorbed — about 20 minutes. Set the rice aside while you finish the stew.

Heat the remaining oil in a large, heavy frying pan over medium-high heat. Add the prawns to the pan and sauté them, stirring, for 2 minutes. Stir in the peppers and celery and cook them for 1 minute. Add the tomatoes, the reserved onion slices and the filé powder if you are using it. Strain the stew base into the frying pan and add the rice. Gently simmer the stew for 5 minutes. Stir in the salt and garnish the stew with the ham, if you are using it, just before serving.

EDITOR'S NOTE: *Filé powder, used to flavour and thicken Creole soups and stews, is made from dried young sassafras leaves.*

Plaice Curry

Serves 4
Working time: about 30 minutes
Total time: about 40 minutes

Calories **280**
Protein **25g**
Cholesterol **55mg**
Total fat **7g**
Saturated fat **1g**
Sodium **205mg**

1 tbsp	chopped fresh ginger root	1 tbsp
½ tsp	turmeric	½ tsp
¼ tsp	ground cumin	¼ tsp
¼ tsp	ground coriander	¼ tsp
⅛ tsp	ground cardamom	⅛ tsp
⅛ tsp	fennel seeds	⅛ tsp
⅛ tsp	ground mace	⅛ tsp
1 tbsp	safflower oil	1 tbsp
2	onions, sliced	2
750 g	ripe tomatoes, skinned, seeded and chopped, or 400 g (14 oz) canned tomatoes, drained and crushed	1½ lb
½ litre	fish stock or unsalted chicken stock	16 fl oz
500 g	mushrooms, wiped clean and halved	1 lb
½	lemon, juice only	½
500 g	plaice fillets (or other white-fleshed fish)	1 lb

Put the ginger, turmeric, cumin, coriander, cardamom, fennel seeds and mace into a mortar; with a pestle, grind the seasonings to a paste. Set the paste aside.

Heat the oil in a large, non-reactive, heavy sauté pan over medium-high heat. Add the onions and sauté them until they are translucent — about 4 minutes. Stir in the spice paste, tomatoes and stock, and bring the liquid to the boil. Add the mushrooms and lemon juice. Lower the heat and simmer the curry until it is reduced by half — 8 to 12 minutes.

Meanwhile, rinse the fillets under cold running water and pat them dry with paper towels. Slice the fillets into 2.5 cm (1 inch) wide strips. Lay the strips on top of the curry, cover the pan, and steam the fish until it is opaque — about 2 minutes. Serve immediately.

Trout Stew with Courgettes, Capers and Watercress

Serves 4
Working time: about 40 minutes
Total time: about 1 hour

Calories **240**
Protein **23g**
Cholesterol **65mg**
Total fat **10g**
Saturated fat **1g**
Sodium **185mg**

1 tbsp	safflower oil	1 tbsp
1	onion, sliced	1
1 tbsp	flour	1 tbsp
12.5 cl	dry white wine	4 fl oz
½ litre	fish stock	16 fl oz
1 tsp	fresh thyme, or ¼ tsp dried thyme	1 tsp
¼ tsp	dry mustard	¼ tsp
350 g	courgettes, quartered lengthwise and cut into strips about 4 cm (1½ inches) long and 5 mm (¼ inch) wide	12 oz
1 tsp	capers, rinsed and drained	1 tsp
500 g	trout fillets	1 lb
4 tbsp	chopped watercress leaves	4 tbsp

Heat the oil in a large, non-reactive, fireproof casserole or heavy pan over medium-high heat. Add the onion slices and sauté them until they are translucent — about 4 minutes. Sprinkle in the flour and stir to coat the onions evenly. Pour in the wine and boil the liquid, stirring, until it is reduced to about 1 tablespoon — approximately 3 minutes. Whisk in the stock, thyme and mustard. Reduce the heat and simmer the mixture, partially covered, for 15 minutes.

Add the courgettes and capers, and continue simmering the mixture until the courgettes are tender — about 5 minutes.

Meanwhile, rinse the trout fillets under cold running water and pat them dry with paper towels, then cut them into 2.5 cm (1 inch) chunks. Arrange the fish pieces on top of the vegetables and cover the casserole. Cook the stew until the fish is opaque — about 3 minutes. Gently stir in the chopped watercress leaves and serve.

Lobster Navarin

ALTHOUGH A TRADITIONAL NAVARIN FEATURES LAMB, THE
FOCAL POINT HERE IS LOBSTER, WHOSE RICH FLAVOUR MAKES
FOR AN EQUALLY SUCCULENT STEW. THE TECHNIQUE OF
"TURNING" VEGETABLES IS SHOWN OVERLEAF.

Serves 2
Working (and total) time: about 1 hour and 30 minutes

Calories **325**
Protein **24g**
Cholesterol **110mg**
Total fat **11g**
Saturated fat **6g**
Sodium **390mg**

1 kg	live lobster	2 lb
15 g	unsalted butter	½ oz
170 g	onion, chopped	6 oz
1 tsp	flour	1 tsp
1	carrot, turned	1
1	turnip, turned	1
1	small cucumber, turned	1
1 tsp	tomato paste	1 tsp
2 tbsp	cognac or Armagnac	2 tbsp
	freshly ground black pepper	
2 tbsp	single cream	2 tbsp

Pour enough water into a pan to fill it about 2.5 cm (1
inch) deep; bring the water to the boil and add the
lobster. Cover the pan and cook the lobster until it

turns a bright red-orange — about 15 minutes.
Remove the lobster from the pan and set it aside until
it is cool enough to handle. Do not discard the liquid.

Working over the pan to catch the juices, twist off
the lobster tail. Snip down either side of the undershell,
then remove the meat in one piece and set it aside. Put
the shells into the pan. Crack the claws; remove the
claw and joint meat, cut it into small pieces, and set it
aside separately from the tail. Put all of the shells into
the pan. Scoop the green tomalley out of the lobster
body and, if desired, reserve it for another use. Hold
the body under cold running water to rinse it out.
Break the body and add it to the pan with the shells.

Pour 1 litre (1¾ pints) of water into the pan and
bring the mixture to the boil. Boil the liquid for 15
minutes, then strain it through a fine sieve into a bowl.
Discard the shells when all of their liquid has drained
into the bowl.

In the pan, melt the butter over medium heat. Add
the onion and cook it until it is translucent — about 5
minutes. Stir in the flour and cook for 1 minute more.
Pour half of the strained lobster liquid back into the
pan. Bring this mixture to the boil, stirring several
times, and continue cooking until almost all of the ▶

liquid has evaporated — about 15 minutes.

Meanwhile, transfer the liquid remaining in the bowl to a small saucepan and bring it to the boil. Add the carrot pieces and cook them for 1½ minutes. Add the turnip pieces and cook for 1½ minutes more, then add the cucumber pieces and continue cooking the vegetables for another 30 seconds. Remove the vegetables with a slotted spoon and set them aside. Do not discard the liquid.

Transfer the reduced onion mixture to a blender or food processor; add the tomato paste and the liquid from the small saucepan, and purée the mixture.

Return the purée to the pan over medium-low heat. Add the claw and joint meat, the turned vegetables, the brandy and some pepper. Cook the navarin until it is heated through — about 4 minutes.

While the navarin heats, slice the tail into eight rounds. Divide the rounds between two serving bowls. Stir the cream into the pan, then spoon the navarin around the lobster in the bowls. Serve immediately.

Turning Vegetables to Elegant Effect

1 *CUTTING A VEGETABLE DOWN TO SIZE. To showcase vegetables, first cut them into rectangles or cylinders about 4 cm (1½ inches) long: for a turnip (below), slice off the top and bottom, then cut the turnip in half. Slice each half into six or eight pieces.*

2 *TURNING THE PIECES. Holding one of the vegetable pieces between your thumb and fingertips, shave off lengthwise strips (above). Rotate the piece and repeat the cut until it resembles an elongated olive. Use trimmings for soup or stock.*

Seafood Chili with Peppers

Serves 4
Working time: about 1 hour and 30 minutes
Total time: about 3 hours and 30 minutes (includes soaking)

Calories **450**
Protein **34g**
Cholesterol **70mg**
Total fat **14g**
Saturated fat **1g**
Sodium **305mg**

185 g	dried black beans, picked over	6½ oz
250 g	queen scallops, rinsed	8 oz
125 g	prawns, peeled	4 oz
125 g	haddock or monkfish fillet, rinsed and cut into pieces about 5 cm (2 inches) long and 2.5 cm (1 inch) wide	4 oz
1	lime, carefully peeled to remove the white pith, sliced into thin rounds	1
1¼ tsp	ground cumin	1¼ tsp
⅛ tsp	ground ginger	⅛ tsp
3¼ tsp	chili powder	3¼ tsp
3 tbsp	coarsely chopped fresh coriander	3 tbsp
2	garlic cloves, finely chopped	2
½	fresh hot green chili pepper, seeded and finely chopped (caution, page 95)	½
3 tbsp	safflower oil	3 tbsp
1	onion, cut into chunks	1
½ tsp	dried tarragon	½ tsp
¼ tsp	salt	¼ tsp
¼ tsp	ground cloves	¼ tsp
⅛ tsp	ground cinnamon	⅛ tsp
⅛ tsp	cayenne pepper	⅛ tsp
35 cl	unsalted chicken stock	12 fl oz
400 g	canned chopped tomatoes, with juice	14 oz
10	small green tomatoes, or 10 husked tomatillos, quartered	10
1	sweet red pepper, seeded, deribbed and cut into chunks the size of the tomato quarters	1
1	sweet yellow pepper, seeded, deribbed and cut into chunks the size of the tomato quarters	1

Rinse the beans under cold running water, then put them into a large pan and pour in enough cold water to cover them by about 7.5 cm (3 inches). Discard any beans that float to the surface. Cover, leaving the lid ajar, and bring the liquid to the boil over medium-low heat. Boil the beans for 2 minutes, then turn off the heat, cover the pan, and soak them for at least 1 hour. (Alternatively, soak the beans overnight in cold water.)

Drain the beans in a colander and return them to the pan. Pour in enough water to cover the beans by about 7.5 cm (3 inches), and bring the liquid to the boil over medium-low heat. Reduce the heat to maintain a strong simmer and cover the pan. Cook the beans, stirring occasionally and skimming any foam from the surface, until they are tender — 1½ to 2 hours.

While the beans are cooking, combine in a large, non-reactive bowl the scallops, prawns, fish pieces, lime, ¼ teaspoon of the cumin, the ginger, ¼ teaspoon of the chili powder, 1 tablespoon of the fresh coriander, half of the garlic, the chili pepper and 1 tablespoon of the oil. Marinate for 30 minutes at room temperature.

While the seafood is marinating, prepare the chili base. Heat 1 tablespoon of the remaining oil in a large, heavy-bottomed saucepan over medium heat. Add the onion and remaining garlic, and cook until the onion is translucent — about 5 minutes. Add the remaining cumin, the remaining chili powder, the tarragon, salt, cloves, cinnamon and cayenne pepper. Cook, stirring constantly, for 2 to 3 minutes to meld the flavours.

Gradually stir in the stock and tomatoes, and bring the mixture to the boil. Reduce the heat to medium low and cover the pan, leaving the lid slightly ajar. Simmer the liquid until it is slightly thickened — 20 to 25 minutes. Drain the beans and add them to the tomato mixture. Set the chili base aside.

Pour the remaining oil into a large, heavy frying pan over high heat. Add the green tomatoes or tomatillos and the pepper chunks, and sauté for 2 minutes. Using a slotted spoon, carefully spread the cooked vegetables over the chili base; bring the mixture to a simmer over low heat. Lay the marinated seafood on top of the vegetables, cover, and steam until the scallops and fish are opaque — 7 to 10 minutes. Sprinkle the remaining coriander over the chili and serve immediately.

EDITOR'S NOTE: *A tomatillo is a small tart green fruit vegetable in the Physalis family. It is not widely available in Europe, but is an authentic ingredient of this dish in Mexico. Warm corn tortillas go well with this chili.*

3 *Ready in minutes, a microwave stew made with mange-tout, lettuce, carrots and courgettes gleams with a sauce of lemon juice and mustard (recipe, opposite).*

Microwaved Soups and Stews

A microwave oven is the ideal vehicle for quick soups and stews, as the recipe for chicken ratatouille on page 138 shows. When cooked in a microwave, the dish requires only about 45 minutes to prepare, and the cooking method preserves the vibrant colours of the vegetables. The microwave oven can also be used to shortcut preparation time for individual ingredients. The squash soup on page 132 would ordinarily have taken much longer to prepare had not the squash been cooked in the microwave first. In a conventional oven, the squash would bake for as long as 1½ hours; in the microwave, it is done in just 13 minutes.

Because microwaving is so quick, flavours may not mingle and meld as they do when soups and stews are cooked conventionally. But there are ways round this dilemma. The seafood stew on page 135 adopts a proven stratagem: a touch of sugar brings unity to the dish. The vegetable stew on this page, a mélange of mange-tout, courgettes, carrots and lettuce — still crisp because the cooking time is only 6 minutes — comes vividly to life through the addition of Dijon mustard.

The microwave offers yet another attraction: summer use. Making a soup or stew in it during the sultry days will not raise the temperature of your kitchen. And when it comes to preparing chilled soups, the microwave can be a special blessing. A perfect example is the cold apple and tarragon soup on page 138, in which ingredients are microwaved for just 6 minutes, then puréed and refrigerated. After only an hour or so, the soup is ready to be garnished with tarragon and served — a cool counterpoint to summer's heat.

Light Vegetable Stew with Mange-Tout and Mustard

Serves 6 as a side dish
Working (and total) time: about 25 minutes

Calories **70**
Protein **2g**
Cholesterol **10mg**
Total fat **4g**
Saturated fat **2g**
Sodium **95mg**

1	courgette, halved lengthwise and cut diagonally into 5 mm (¼ inch) thick slices	1
1 tbsp	fresh lemon juice	1 tbsp
30 g	unsalted butter, cut into pieces	1 oz
2	carrots, cut diagonally into 5 mm (¼ inch) thick ovals	2
1	shallot, finely chopped	1
1 tbsp	Dijon mustard	1 tbsp
1	cos lettuce, cored, the leaves torn into 5 cm (2 inch) pieces	1
1 tsp	fresh thyme, or ¼ tsp dried thyme	1 tsp
⅛ tsp	salt	⅛ tsp
	freshly ground black pepper	
125 g	mange-tout, any stems and strings removed, large pods halved diagonally	4 oz

Put the courgette slices into a small bowl, toss them with the lemon juice, and set the bowl aside.

Put the butter into a large bowl and microwave it on high until it melts — about 1 minute. Stir in the carrots, shallot and mustard. Cook the mixture on high for 2 minutes, stirring half way through the cooking time.

Add the lettuce, thyme, salt and some pepper; stir the vegetables to coat them with the butter. Microwave the stew on high for 1 minute, stirring once after 30 seconds. Stir in the courgette slices and lemon juice, then the mange-tout. Cook the stew on high for 3 minutes more, stirring once half way through the cooking time. Stir the vegetables one last time, cover the bowl and let the stew stand for another 3 minutes before serving it.

Gingery Squash Soup

Serves 4
Working time: about 15 minutes
Total time: about 25 minutes

Calories **95**
Protein **3g**
Cholesterol **5mg**
Total fat **4g**
Saturated fat **2g**
Sodium **185mg**

750 g	acorn or other squash	1½ lb
10 g	unsalted butter	⅓ oz
1	small onion, finely chopped	1
1	garlic clove, finely chopped	1
1	small carrot, very thinly sliced	1
35 cl	unsalted chicken stock	12 fl oz
6 cl	semi-skimmed milk	2 fl oz
½ tsp	ground ginger	½ tsp
¼ tsp	salt	¼ tsp
⅛ tsp	white pepper	⅛ tsp
1 tsp	toasted sesame seeds (optional)	1 tsp

Put the squash in a shallow 20 by 25 cm (8 by 10 inch) glass baking dish and microwave it on high for 30 seconds. Remove the squash from the oven; when the squash is cool enough to handle, cut off the stem, then halve the squash lengthwise. Spoon out the seeds and place the squash halves cut sides down in the dish. Cover the dish and microwave the squash on high for 7 minutes. Let the squash stand, covered, for 5 minutes.

Put the butter in a bowl and cover the bowl with plastic film or a lid; microwave the butter on high for 45 seconds. Stir the onion, garlic and carrot into the butter, then cover the bowl and microwave it on medium (50 per cent power) for 4 minutes more. With a spoon, carefully scoop the squash flesh into the bowl; pour in the stock and cook the mixture on high, covered, for 2½ minutes. Stir the mixture and cook it on high for 2½ minutes more.

Transfer the vegetables and stock to a food processor or blender. Pour in the milk and purée the mixture, stopping occasionally to scrape down the sides. Stir in the ginger, salt and pepper. Reheat if cooled, then transfer the soup to a serving bowl; garnish it with the sesame seeds if you are using them.

Sweet-and-Sour Fish Stew

Serves 4
Working (and total) time: about 50 minutes

Calories **215**
Protein **25g**
Cholesterol **40mg**
Total fat **1g**
Saturated fat **0g**
Sodium **175mg**

2	carrots, julienned	2
4	spring onions, trimmed and cut into 1 cm (½ inch) lengths	4
1 tbsp	finely chopped fresh ginger root	1 tbsp
¼ tsp	dark sesame oil	¼ tsp
½ litre	fish stock	16 fl oz
1 tbsp	sugar	1 tbsp
2 tbsp	cornflour, mixed with 3 tbsp water	2 tbsp
2 tbsp	rice vinegar or white wine vinegar	2 tbsp
1 tsp	sweet chili sauce, or ½ tsp crushed hot red pepper flakes mixed with 1 tsp golden syrup and ½ tsp vinegar	1 tsp
1 tsp	low-sodium soy sauce or shoyu	1 tsp
4	dried shiitake or Chinese black mushrooms, soaked in boiling water for 15 minutes, stemmed and cut into strips	4
500 g	cod, bass or monkfish fillet, rinsed and cut into 2.5 cm (1 inch) cubes	1 lb
125 g	mange-tout, strings and stems removed	4 oz
75 g	drained and rinsed bamboo shoots	2½ oz
30 g	cellophane noodles, soaked in ½ litre (16 fl oz) hot water for 10 minutes, drained and cut into 5 cm (2 inch) lengths	1 oz

Combine the carrots, spring onions, ginger and oil in a 2 litre (3½ pint) glass bowl. Cover and microwave on medium (50 per cent power) for 3 minutes. Stir in the stock, sugar, cornflour mixture, vinegar, chili sauce or pepper flake mixture, soy sauce and mushrooms. Cover, and cook on high for 3 minutes.

Arrange the fish cubes in a single layer in a shallow baking dish. Distribute the mange-tout, bamboo shoots and noodles on top of the fish. Pour the sweet-and-sour sauce over all, cover, and microwave on high for 2 minutes. Rearrange the fish, moving less-cooked cubes from the centre of the dish to the edges. Cover once more and cook on high until the fish can be easily flaked with a fork — about 2 minutes.

EDITOR'S NOTE: *Cellophane noodles and bamboo shoots are available from Asian food shops.*

Pork and Bean Sprout Soup

Serves 4
Working time: about 30 minutes
Total time: about 1 hour

Calories **245**
Protein **30g**
Cholesterol **75mg**
Total fat **5g**
Saturated fat **2g**
Sodium **490mg**

½ tsp	Sichuan peppercorns, or freshly ground black pepper to taste	½ tsp
500 g	lean pork, julienned	1 lb
¼ tsp	cayenne pepper	¼ tsp
¼ tsp	ground ginger	¼ tsp
2 tbsp	Chinese black vinegar or balsamic vinegar	2 tbsp
1 litre	unsalted brown stock	1¾ pints
1	onion, thinly sliced	1
6	garlic cloves, thinly sliced	6
250 g	bean sprouts	8 oz
1.25 kg	ripe tomatoes, skinned, seeded and chopped, or 800 g (28 oz) canned tomatoes, drained and crushed	2½ lb
4 tbsp	chopped fresh parsley	4 tbsp
2 tbsp	low-sodium soy sauce or shoyu	2 tbsp

Toast the Sichuan peppercorns, if you are using them, in a heavy frying pan over medium-high heat until they smoke — about 2 minutes; using a mortar and pestle, grind them to a powder. Combine the pork with the ground peppercorns or black pepper, cayenne pepper, ginger and vinegar in a small bowl. Let the mixture stand at room temperature for 30 minutes.

Pour the stock into a 2 litre (3½ pint) glass bowl. Add the onion and garlic, and cover the bowl with a lid. Microwave the liquid on high for 10 minutes. Remove the bowl from the oven and stir the mixture. Cover the bowl again and cook the liquid on high for 10 minutes more.

Meanwhile, place the bean sprouts in a colander and blanch them by pouring about 2 litres (3½ pints) of boiling water over them. Set the bean sprouts aside.

Stir the pork and its marinade into the cooked broth. Microwave the mixture on high until it barely begins to boil, then cook on high for 3 minutes. Add the tomatoes, parsley, soy sauce and blanched bean sprouts. Cook the soup, uncovered, for 3 minutes more on high. Serve immediately.

Seafood Stew in Garlic-Tomato Sauce

Serves 6
Working (and total) time: about 1 hour

Calories **220**
Protein **24g**
Cholesterol **175mg**
Total fat **5g**
Saturated fat **1g**
Sodium **305mg**

1 kg	mussels, scrubbed and debearded	2 lb
12.5 cl	dry white wine	4 fl oz
1 tsp	chopped fresh oregano, or ¼ tsp dried oregano	1 tsp
	freshly ground black pepper	
175 g	squid, cleaned	6 oz
500 g	cooked prawns, peeled	1 lb
Garlic-tomato sauce		
1	onion, chopped	1
4	garlic cloves, finely chopped	4
1 tsp	chopped fresh oregano, or ¼ tsp dried oregano	1 tsp
⅛ tsp	cayenne pepper	⅛ tsp
1	lime, juice only	1
1 tsp	caster sugar	1 tsp
1 tbsp	virgin olive oil	1 tbsp
1.25 kg	ripe tomatoes, skinned, seeded and chopped, or 800 g (28 oz) canned tomatoes, drained and chopped	2½ lb
1	sweet green pepper, seeded, deribbed and cut into thin strips	1

Place half of the mussels, along with the wine, oregano and some black pepper, in a 2 litre (3½ pint) bowl. Cover the bowl with plastic film (leaving one corner open) or a lid and microwave the mussels on high, rotating the dish half way through the cooking time,

until they open — about 5 minutes. Remove the opened mussels and set them aside; discard any that remain closed. Cook the other half of the mussels in the same way. Do not pour out the cooking liquid.

When the mussels are cool enough to handle, remove them from their shells, working over the bowl to catch their juices. Discard the shells and set the mussels aside. Strain the liquid through a sieve lined with muslin into a cup; discard the solids. Wash the cooking bowl in order to make the sauce in it.

To make the garlic-tomato sauce, put the onion, ▶

garlic, oregano, cayenne pepper, lime juice, sugar and oil into the bowl. Cover it and cook the mixture on high for 2 minutes. Add the tomatoes and the reserved liquid from the mussels and cook, covered, on high for 10 minutes, stirring half way through the cooking time. Reduce the heat to medium (50 per cent power) and cook the sauce for 10 minutes more, again stirring after 5 minutes.

While the sauce is cooking, prepare the squid. Slit one side of the pouch and lay it flat, skinned side down. Using a sharp knife, score the flesh diagonally in a crosshatch pattern. Then cut the pouch into 4 cm (1½ inch) squares and set them aside.

Add the green pepper to the sauce and continue to cook the mixture on medium (50 per cent power) until the pepper is tender — about 5 minutes. Stir in the mussels, squid and prawns. Cook the dish on high for an additional 2 minutes and serve it hot.

Chicken Stew with Mashed Potatoes

Serves 4
Working time: about 25 minutes
Total time: about 50 minutes

Calories **355**
Protein **25g**
Cholesterol **70mg**
Total fat **9g**
Saturated fat **3g**
Sodium **330mg**

1 kg	chicken drumsticks, skinned	2 lb
	freshly ground black pepper	
¼ tsp	paprika, preferably Hungarian	¼ tsp
1	garlic clove, finely chopped	1
1	small onion, cut into 2 cm (¾ inch) pieces	1
2	small carrots, cut into 1 cm (½ inch) pieces	2
2	sticks celery, thinly sliced	2
1	bay leaf	1
¼ tsp	salt	¼ tsp
½ tsp	fresh thyme, or ⅛ tsp dried thyme	½ tsp
2 tbsp	cornflour, mixed with 2 tbsp water	2 tbsp
Mashed potatoes		
750 g	small potatoes	1½ lb
2 tsp	finely cut chives or green spring onion tops	2 tsp
⅛ tsp	salt	⅛ tsp
⅛ tsp	white pepper	⅛ tsp
	grated nutmeg	
17.5 cl	semi-skimmed milk, warmed	6 fl oz

To prepare the mashed potatoes, first prick each potato several times with a fork. Arrange the potatoes around the edge of a plate. Microwave them on high for 10 minutes, stopping half way through the cooking to turn the potatoes over. Remove the potatoes from the oven and set them aside.

Sprinkle the chicken drumsticks with some pepper and the paprika. Arrange the drumsticks in a single layer in a large, shallow baking dish; the meatier portions of the drumsticks should face outwards. Place the garlic, onion, and carrot and celery pieces between the drumsticks. Pour in 35 cl (12 fl oz) of water, then add the bay leaf, salt and thyme. Cover the dish with a lid. Microwave the chicken on high for 12 minutes, stopping after 6 minutes to turn the drumsticks over.

While the chicken is cooking, cut the cooled potatoes in half and spoon out the flesh into a bowl. Discard the skins. Use a food mill or a potato masher to mash the potatoes. Add the chives or green spring onion tops, salt, white pepper and a small pinch of nutmeg, then whisk in the warmed milk. Transfer the potatoes to a piping bag fitted with a large star tube.

Remove the dish with the chicken from the oven. Stir the cornflour mixture into the liquid in the dish. Using the piping bag, pipe a decorative band of potatoes down the centre of the dish. Return the dish to the oven and cook it on high for 2 minutes more.

Broccoli Soup with Cumin and Scallops

Serves 8
Working time: about 20 minutes
Total time: about 50 minutes

Calories **140**
Protein **8g**
Cholesterol **30mg**
Total fat **7g**
Saturated fat **4g**
Sodium **280mg**

30 g	unsalted butter	1 oz
500 g	broccoli, florets cut off, stems peeled and cut into 2.5 cm (1 inch) lengths	1 lb
2	leeks, split, washed thoroughly to remove all grit, and thinly sliced	2
1	large potato, peeled and cut into 1 cm (½ inch) pieces	1
1	garlic clove, finely chopped	1
2 tsp	fresh thyme, or ½ tsp dried thyme	2 tsp
	freshly ground black pepper	
¾ tsp	salt	¾ tsp
1 litre	unsalted chicken stock	1¾ pints
¾ tsp	ground cumin	¾ tsp
2 tbsp	fresh lemon juice	2 tbsp
12.5 cl	single cream	4 fl oz
250 g	queen scallops, firm white connective tissue removed	8 oz

Put half of the butter into a 4 litre (7 pint) casserole. Add the broccoli, leeks, potato, garlic, thyme and some pepper. Cover the casserole with a lid or plastic film, then microwave the vegetables on high for 5 minutes.

Add the salt, stock, ¾ litre (1¼ pints) of water and the cumin. Cover the dish leaving a corner open for the steam to escape, then microwave the mixture on high for 15 minutes, stirring every 5 minutes. Stir in the lemon juice and cook the mixture on high for 15 minutes more, stirring every 5 minutes. Let the casserole stand for 10 minutes before puréeing the mixture in batches in a blender or food processor. Return the purée to the casserole; then stir in the cream. Microwave the mixture on high until it is heated through — about 2 minutes.

In a bowl, microwave the remaining butter on high until it melts — about 30 seconds. Add the scallops and cook them on high for 30 seconds; stir the scallops, then cook them just until they turn opaque — about 30 seconds more.

Ladle the hot purée into heated individual soup plates; garnish each serving with some scallops and serve the soup immediately.

Cold Apple and Tarragon Soup

Serves 4
Working (and total) time: about 1 hour and 20 minutes
(includes chilling)

Calories **150**
Protein **4g**
Cholesterol **10mg**
Total fat **4g**
Saturated fat **2g**
Sodium **130mg**

7 g	unsalted butter	¼ oz
1 tbsp	finely chopped shallot	1 tbsp
600 g	tart apples, peeled, cored and sliced	1¼ lb
2 tbsp	chopped fresh tarragon	2 tbsp
30 cl	unsalted chicken stock	½ pint
17.5 cl	unsweetened apple juice	6 fl oz
¼ tsp	white pepper	¼ tsp
⅛ tsp	salt	⅛ tsp
	grated nutmeg	
¼ litre	semi-skimmed milk	8 fl oz
	tarragon sprigs for garnish (optional)	

Put the butter into a 2 litre (3½ pint) bowl. Cover the bowl with plastic film or a lid, and microwave the butter on high until it has melted — about 30 seconds. Add the shallot and stir to coat it with the butter. Cover the bowl again and cook the shallot on medium high (70 per cent power) until it is translucent — about 45 seconds. Add the apples, tarragon, stock, apple juice, pepper, salt and a pinch of nutmeg. Cover the bowl, leaving one corner open, and cook the mixture on high until the apples are soft — about 6 minutes.

Purée the contents of the bowl in a blender, food processor or food mill. Return the soup to the bowl and refrigerate it for at least 1 hour, then stir in the milk. Garnish the soup with the tarragon sprigs, if you are using them, and serve immediately.

Chicken Ratatouille

Serves 4
Working (and total) time: about 45 minutes

Calories **240**
Protein **29g**
Cholesterol **70mg**
Total fat **5g**
Saturated fat **1g**
Sodium **345mg**

4 tbsp	Madeira	4 tbsp
2 tsp	chopped fresh oregano, or ½ tsp dried oregano	2 tsp
1 tsp	chopped fresh rosemary, or ½ tsp dried rosemary	1 tsp
1 tsp	chopped fresh thyme, or ¼ tsp dried thyme	1 tsp
2 tbsp	finely chopped shallot	2 tbsp
2	garlic cloves, finely chopped	2
1 tsp	safflower oil	1 tsp
400 g	canned tomatoes, puréed with their juice in a blender or food processor	14 oz
1	small bay leaf	1
350 g	aubergine, cut into 2.5 cm (1 inch) chunks	12 oz
2	small courgettes (preferably 1 green and 1 yellow), cut into 2.5 cm (1 inch) chunks	2
1	sweet red pepper, seeded, deribbed and cut into 2.5 cm (1 inch) squares	1
1	sweet green pepper, seeded, deribbed and cut into 2.5 cm (1 inch) squares	1
½ tsp	salt	½ tsp
	freshly ground black pepper	
500 g	chicken breast meat, cut into 2 cm (¾ inch) cubes	1 lb

Place the Madeira, oregano, rosemary and thyme in a cup and microwave them on high for 2 minutes. Set the cup aside and let it stand for 5 minutes.

Put the shallot and garlic into a 2 litre (3½ pint) glass bowl; stir in the oil and microwave the mixture on medium (50 per cent power) for 2 minutes. Add the tomato purée, bay leaf, aubergine, courgettes, red pepper, green pepper and the herb mixture. Stir gently to distribute the vegetables, then cover the bowl with plastic film or a lid. Microwave the mixture on high for 8 minutes, stirring once during the process.

Sprinkle the salt and some pepper over the chicken cubes, then stir them into the ratatouille. Cover the bowl and microwave it on high for 5 minutes, stirring once during the process. If the chicken is not white throughout, cook the ratatouille for 1 or 2 minutes more. Remove the bay leaf and transfer the ratatouille to a warmed serving dish. Serve immediately.

Glossary

Balsamic vinegar: a mild, extremely fragrant wine-based vinegar made in northern Italy.
Bâtonnet (also called bâton): a vegetable piece that has been cut in the shape of a stick; bâtonnets are slightly larger than julienne.
Bean curd: see Tofu.
Bean paste: see Soya bean paste.
Blanch: to partially cook food by briefly immersing it in boiling water. Blanching makes thin-skinned fruits and vegetables easier to peel; it can also mellow strong flavours.
Bok choy (also called Chinese chard): a sweet-tasting cruciferous vegetable that grows in a celery-like bunch, with smooth white stalks and wide, dark-green leaves.
Bouquet garni: several herbs — the classic three are parsley, thyme and bay leaf — tied together or wrapped in muslin and used to flavour a stock or stew. The bouquet garni is removed and discarded at the end of the cooking time.
Buttermilk: a tangy, low-fat cultured-milk product that can be used in cooking to replace richer ingredients.
Calorie (kilocalorie): a precise measure of the energy food supplies when it is broken down for use in the body.
Caramelize: to heat sugar, or a naturally sugar-rich food such as onion, until the sugar becomes brown and syrupy.
Cardamom: the bittersweet aromatic dried seeds or whole pods of a plant in the ginger family. Often used in curries.
Casserole: a heavy, heat-absorbing pot, ideal for cooking soups and stews slowly. To prevent evaporation of the liquid, the casserole should have a tight lid. Only fireproof casseroles made specifically for the purpose should be used on top of the stove.
Cayenne pepper: a fiery powder ground from the seeds and pods of various red chili peppers.
Celeriac (also called celery root): the knobby, tuberous root of a plant in the celery family.
Cellophane noodles (also called bean-thread noodles, glass noodles, *harusame, saifun* and transparent noodles): an Asian pasta made from various vegetable starches, most often that of mung beans. Cellophane noodles are available in forms ranging from small skeins to 500 g (1 lb) packages of loose noodles. Before cooking they should be soaked in hot water until they are soft.
Chervil: a lacy, slightly anise-flavoured herb. Because long cooking may kill its flavour, chervil should be added at the last minute.
Chili paste: a paste of chili peppers, salt and other ingredients, among them garlic and black beans. Several kinds are available in Asian shops.
Chili peppers: a variety of hot red or green peppers. Serranos and jalepeños are small fresh green chilies that are extremely hot. Anchos are dried poblano chilies that are mildly hot and dark red in colour. Fresh or dried, chili peppers contain volatile oils that can irritate the skin and eyes; they must be handled with extreme care (caution, page 95). See also Chili paste.
Chinese cabbage (also called Chinese leaves): an elongated cabbage resembling cos lettuce, with long broad ribs and crinkled, light green to white leaves.

Chinese chard: see Bok choy.
Chinese five-spice powder (also called five heavenly spices and five fragrant spices): a pungent blend of ground spices, most often fennel seeds, star anise, cloves, cinnamon or cassia, and Sichuan peppercorns; it should be used sparingly. If five-spice powder is unavailable, substitute a mixture of equal parts ground Sichuan peppercorns, cloves, cinnamon and fennel seeds.
Cholesterol: a wax-like substance manufactured in the human body and also found in foods of animal origin. Although a certain amount of cholesterol is necessary for proper body functioning, an excess can accumulate in the arteries, contributing to heart disease. See also Monounsaturated fats; Polyunsaturated fats; Saturated fats.
Coriander (also called cilantro): the pungent peppery leaves of the coriander plant or its earthy tasting seeds. It is a common seasoning in Middle-Eastern, Oriental and Latin-American cookery.
Cloud-ear mushrooms (also called tree ears, tree fungus, mo-er and wood ears): flavourless lichen used primarily for their crunchy texture and dark colour. Cloud ears expand more than other mushrooms when soaked. See also Mushrooms, dried Asian.
Coconut milk, unsweetened: a liquid extracted from fresh or dried coconut meat. Unsweetened coconut milk can be purchased either canned or frozen; because of its high saturated fat content, it should be used sparingly.
Couscous: cereal processed from semolina into pellets, traditionally steamed and served with meat and vegetables in the classic North African stew of the same name.
Crystallized ginger (also called candied ginger): stems of young ginger preserved with sugar. Crystallized ginger should not be confused with ginger in syrup.
Cumin: the aromatic seeds of an unbelliferous plant similar to fennel used, whole or powdered, as a spice, especially in Indian and Latin-American dishes. Toasting gives it a nutty flavour.
Dark sesame oil: a dark seasoning oil, high in polyunsaturated fats, that is made from toasted sesame seeds. Because the oil has a low smoking point, it is rarely heated. Dark sesame oil should not be confused or replaced with lighter sesame cooking oils.
Deglaze: to dissolve the brown particles left in a pan after roasting or sautéing by stirring in a liquid such as wine, stock, water or cream.
Degrease: to remove fat from the surface of stock or a cooking liquid. See also box, page 55.
Dice: to cut a food into small cubes of equal size.
Dijon mustard: a smooth or grainy mustard once manufactured only in Dijon, France; may be flavoured with herbs, green peppercorns or white wine.
Fennel: a herb (also called wild fennel) whose feathery leaves and dried seeds have a mild anise flavour and are much used for flavouring. Its vegetable relative, the bulb — or Florence — fennel (also called finocchio) can be cooked, or eaten raw in salads.
Fermented black beans: soya beans that have been cured in salt, sometimes with citrus peel; used in Chinese dishes. To remove their excess salt, rinse the beans before use.

Fish sauce (also called *nuoc mam* and *nam pla*): a thin, brown, salty liquid made from fermented fish and used in South-East Asian cooking to bring out the flavours of a dish.
Ginger: the spicy, buff-coloured, root of the ginger plant, used as a seasoning either fresh, or dried in powder form. See also Crystallized ginger.
Harissa: a fiery-hot North African condiment, based on red chili peppers. Sambal oelek (see below) may be used in its place.
Hoisin sauce: a thick, dark reddish brown, soya bean-based Chinese condiment. Its flavour is at once sweet and spicy.
Hot red-pepper sauce: a hot, unsweetened chili sauce, such as Tabasco sauce.
Julienne: the French term for vegetables or other food cut into strips.
Juniper berries: the berries of the juniper tree, used as the key flavouring in gin as well as in pork dishes and sauerkraut. Whole berries should be removed from a dish before it is served.
Lemon grass (citronella): a long, woody, lemon-flavoured stalk that is shaped like a spring onion. Lemon grass is available in Asian shops. To store it, refrigerate it in plastic film for up to two weeks or freeze it for as long as three months.
Mange-tout: flat green pea pods eaten whole, with only stems and strings removed.
Mirin: a sweet Japanese cooking wine that is made from rice. If mirin is unavailable, substitute white wine or sake mixed with a little sugar.
Monounsaturated fats: one of the three types of fats found in foods. Monounsaturated fats are believed not to raise the level of cholesterol in the blood.
Mushrooms, dried Asian: any of several fungi often used in Asian cooking. Before use, dried Asian mushrooms must be covered with boiling water and soaked for at least 20 minutes, then trimmed of their woody stems. To convert the mushroom-soaking liquid into a flavouring agent, let the sand settle out, then pour off and reserve the clear liquid. See also Cloud-ear mushrooms; Shiitake mushrooms.
Non-reactive pan: a cooking vessel whose surface does not chemically react with food. Materials used include stainless steel, enamel, glass and some alloys. Untreated cast iron and aluminium may react with acids, producing discoloration or a peculiar taste.
Okra: the green pods of a plant indigenous to Africa, where it is called gumbo. In stews, okra is prized for its thickening properties.
Olive oil: any of various grades of oil extracted from olives. Extra virgin olive oil has a full, fruity flavour and the lowest acidity. Virgin olive oil is slightly higher in acidity. Pure olive oil, a processed blend of olive oils, has the highest acidity and the lightest taste.
Orzo: a rice-shaped pasta made from semolina.
Poach: to cook a food in barely simmering liquid.
Polyunsaturated fats: one of the three types of fats found in foods. They exist in abundance in such vegetable oils as safflower, sunflower, corn and soya bean. Polyunsaturated fats lower the level of cholesterol in the blood.
Purée: to reduce food to a smooth, even, pulp-like consistency by mashing it, passing it through a sieve,

or processing it in a blender or food processor.

Puréed tomatoes: purée made from skinned fresh or canned tomatoes. Available commercially, but should not be confused with the thicker, concentrated tomato paste sometimes labelled tomato purée.

Recommended Daily Amount (RDA): the average daily amount of an essential nutrient recommended for healthy people by the U.K. Department of Health and Social Security.

Reduce: to boil down a liquid in order to concentrate its flavour or thicken its consistency.

Rice vinegar: a mild, fragrant vinegar that is less sweet than cider vinegar and not as harsh as distilled white vinegar. Japanese rice vinegar is milder than the Chinese variety.

Rice wine: Chinese rice wine *(shao-hsing)* is brewed from rice and wine. Japanese rice wine (sake) has a different flavour but may be used as a substitute. If rice wine is not available, use sherry in its place. See also Mirin.

Ricotta: soft, mild, white Italian cheese, made from cow's or sheep's milk. Full-fat ricotta has a fat content of 20 to 30 per cent, but the low-fat ricotta used in the recipes in this book has a fat content of only about 8 per cent.

Rocket (also called arugula): a peppery flavoured salad plant with long, leafy stems, popular in Italy.

Roll-cut: to slice a cylindrical vegetable, such as a carrot or an asparagus stalk, by rolling it a quarter of a turn between diagonal slices. The decorative pieces that result offer increased surface area for seasonings.

Safflower oil: vegetable oil that contains the highest proportion of polyunsaturated fats.

Saffron: the dried, yellowish-red stigmas (or threads) of the saffron crocus, which yield a powerful yellow colour as well as a pungent flavour. Powdered saffron may be substituted for the threads but has less flavour.

Sake: Japanese rice wine.

Sambal oelek: an Indonesian chili paste.

Saturated fats: one of the three types of fats found in food. They exist in abundance in animal products and coconut and palm oils; they raise the level of cholesterol in the blood. Because high blood-cholesterol levels may cause heart disease, saturated fat consumption should be restricted to less than 15 per cent of the calories provided by the daily diet.

Savoy cabbage: a variety of head cabbage with a mild flavour and crisp, crinkly leaves.

Scallop: a bivalve mollusc found throughout the world, in the Atlantic from Iceland to Spain and in the Pacific from Alaska to Australia. The white nut of meat (actually the adductor muscle) and the orange roe, or coral, are eaten. Tiny queen scallops are a different species from the familiar large scallops known in France as *coquilles Saint-Jacques.*

Sesame oil: see Dark sesame oil.

Sesame seeds: pale seeds of the sesame plant that are a good source of calcium. To toast sesame seeds, cook them in a dry pan over low heat, stirring or shaking the pan gently to prevent burning, until the seeds are golden.

Shallot: a mild variety of onion, with a subtle flavour and papery, red-brown skin.

Shiitake mushrooms: a variety of mushroom, originally cultivated only in Japan, that is sold fresh or dried. The dried form should be soaked and stemmed before use. See also Mushrooms, dried Asian.

Shoyu: see Soy sauce.

Sichuan pepper (also called Chinese pepper, Japanese pepper and anise pepper): the dried berry of a shrub native to China. Its flavour is tart, aromatic and less piquant than that of black pepper. To toast Sichuan peppercorns, cook them in a dry pan over low heat, gently shaking the pan to prevent burning, until the peppercorns are fragrant.

Simmer: to cook a liquid or sauce just below its boiling point so that the liquid's surface barely trembles.

Sodium: a nutrient essential to maintaining the proper balance of fluids in the body. In most diets, a major source of the element is table salt, made up of 40 per cent sodium. Excess sodium may contribute to high blood pressure, which increases the risk of heart disease. One teaspoon (5.5 g) of salt, with 2,132 milligrams of sodium, contains just over the maximum daily amount that is recommended by the World Health Organization.

Soy sauce: a savoury, salty, brown liquid made from fermented soya beans. One tablespoon of ordinary soy sauce contains 1,030 milligrams of sodium; lower-sodium variations, such as naturally fermented shoyu, used in the recipes in this book, may contain as little as half that amount.

Soya bean paste (also called miso): a thick brown paste made from fermented soya beans, spices and salt.

Stock: a savoury liquid made by simmering aromatic vegetables, herbs and spices — and usually meat, bones and trimmings — in water *(recipes, pages 10-11).* Stock forms a flavour-rich base for soups and stews.

Sweet chili sauce: any of a group of Asian sauces containing chilies, vinegar, garlic, sugar and salt. The sauce may be used as a condiment to accompany meats, poultry or fish, or it may be included as an ingredient in a dish.

Tabasco sauce: a hot, unsweetened chili sauce. A similar Asian version is the Thai *sriracha* sauce.

Tamarind (also called Indian date): the pulp surrounding the seeds of the tarmarind plant, yielding a juice considerably more sour than lemon juice. Grown and used throughout Asia, it is available fresh, in pod form, in bricks or as a concentrate.

Tarragon: a strong herb with a sweet anise taste. Iin combination with other herbs — notably sage, rosemary and thyme — it should be used sparingly to avoid a clash of flavours. Because heat intensifies the herb's flavour, cooked dishes require smaller amounts of tarragon.

Thyme: a versatile herb with a zesty, slightly fruity flavour, and strong aroma.

Tofu (also called bean curd): a dense, unfermented soya bean product with a mild flavour. It is rich in protein, relatively low in calories and free of cholesterol.

Tomato paste: a concentrated tomato purée, available in cans and tubes, used in sauces and soups. See also Puréed tomatoes.

Total fat: an individual's daily intake of polyunsaturated, monounsaturated and saturated fats. Nutritionists recommend that fats provide no more than 35 per cent of the energy in the diet. The term as used in this book refers to the combined fats in a given dish or food.

Turmeric: a spice used as a colouring agent and occasionally as a substitute for saffron. It has a musty odour and a slightly bitter flavour.

Virgin olive oil: see Olive oil.

Water chestnut: the walnut-sized tuber of an aquatic Asian plant, with rough brown skin and sweet, crisp white flesh. Fresh water chestnuts may be refrigerated for up to two weeks; they must be peeled before use. To store canned water chestnuts, first blanch or rinse them, then refrigerate them for no longer than three weeks in fresh water changed daily.

White pepper: a powder ground from the same dried berry as that used to make black pepper, but with the berry's outer shell removed before grinding, resulting in a milder flavour. Ground white pepper is used as a less visible alternative to black pepper in light-coloured foods.

Yogurt: a smooth-textured, semi-solid cultured milk product made with varying percentages of fat. Yogurt makes an excellent substitute for soured cream in cooking. Yogurt may also be combined with soured cream to produce a sauce or topping that is lower in fat and calories than soured cream alone.

Index

Picture Credits

All photographs in this volume were taken by staff photographer Renée Comet unless otherwise indicated below.

Cover: James Murphy. 2: top and centre, Carolyn Wall Rothery. 5: lower right, Taran Z. 9: Taran Z. 16: below, Michael Latil. 20: Steven Biver. 23: above, Michael Latil. 25: Steven Biver. 31,32: Michael Latil. 33: Aldo Tutino. 37: above, Michael Latil. 38-43: Steven Biver. 45: Steven Biver. 49: above, Michael Latil; bottom, Taran Z. 50-51: Taran Z. 55: Taran Z. 57: Michael Latil. 61: above, Michael Latil. 63: Michael Latil. 68: John Elliott. 70: Michael Latil. 71: John Elliott. 90, 91: Michael Latil. 93: Michael Latil. 97: Taran Z. 103-105: Michael Latil. 107: Taran Z. 109: Michael Latil. 112: upper left, Taran Z; lower left, Michael Latil. 114-115: Taran Z. 118: Taran Z. 121: Michael Latil. 123: Michael Latil. 125: Michael Latil. 127, 128: Taran Z. 130: Taran Z. 133, 134: Taran Z. 136-138: Taran Z.

Acknowledgements

The editors are particularly indebted to the following people: Mary Jane Blandford, Alexandria, Va., U.S.A.; Leslie Bloom, Silver Spring, Md., U.S.A.; Ellen Brown, Washington, D. C.; Nora Carey, Paris; Robert Carmack, Camas, Wash., U.S.A.; Robert Chambers, New York; Sharon Farrington, Bethesda, Md., U.S.A.; Carol Gvozdich and Nancy Lendved, Alexandria, Va., U.S.A.; Rebecca Marshall, New York; Vivian Portner, Silver Spring, Md., U.S.A.; Tajvana Queen, Alexandria, Va., U.S.A.; Ann Ready, Alexandria, Va., U.S.A.; Christine Schuyler, Washington, D.C.; Jane Sigal, Paris; Lyn Stallworth, Brooklyn, N.Y.; Rita Walters, London; Sarah Wiley, London; Ci Ci Williamson, Alexandria, Va., U.S.A.

The editors also wish to thank: The Amber Grain, Washington, D.C.; Ava Baker, Walpole, Mass., U.S.A.; Moira Banks, London; Martha Blacksall, BBH Corporation, Washington, D.C.; Jo Calabrese, Royal Worcester Spode Inc., New York; Nick Chantiles, Rockville, Md., U.S.A.; Nic Colling, Home Produce Company, Alexandria, Va., U.S.A.; Jeanne Dale, The Pilgrim Glass Corp., New York; Paul Dexter, Salvatore Termini, Deruta of Italy Corp., New York; Rex Downey, Oxon Hill, Md., U.S.A.; Dr. Jacob Exler, U.S. Department of Agriculture, Hyattsville, Md., U.S.A.; Flowers Unique, Alexandria, Va., U.S.A.; Dennis Garrett, Ed Nash, The American Hand Plus, Washington, D.C.; Giant Food, Inc., Landover, Md., U.S.A.; E. Goodwin & Sons, Inc., Jessup, Md., U.S.A.; Chong Su Han, Grass Roots Restaurant, Alexandria, Va., U.S.A.; Wretha Hanson, Franz Bader Gallery, Washingon, D.C.; Steven Himmelfarb, U.S. Fish, Inc., Kensington, Md., U.S.A.; Imperial Produce, Washington, D.C.; Ann Kavaljian, Alexandria, Va., U.S.A.; Gary Latzman, Kirk Phillips, Retroneu, New York; Patricia Cassidy Lewis, Lorton, Va., U.S.A.; Dr. Richard Mattes, Monell Chemical Senses Center, Philadelphia, Pa., U.S.A.; Nambé Mills Inc., Santa Fe, N. Mex., U.S.A.; Dr. Joyce Nettleton, Lexington, Mass., U.S.A.; Dr. Alfred C. Olson, U.S. Department of Agriculture, Albany, Calif., U.S.A.; Lisa Ownby, Alexandria, Va., U.S.A.; Joyce Piotrowski, Vienna, Va., U.S.A.; Linda Robertson, JUD Tile, Vienna, Va., U.S.A.; Safeway Stores, Inc., Landover, Md., U.S.A.; St. John's Herb Garden, Inc., Bowie, Md., U.S.A.; Bert Saunders, WILTON Armetale, New York; Straight from the Crate, Inc., Alexandria, Va., U.S.A.; Sutton Place Gourmet, Washington, D.C.; Kathy Swekel, Columbia, Md., U.S.A.; Williams-Sonoma, Washington, D.C.
The Editors wish to thank the following for their donation of kitchen equipment: Le Creuset, distributed by Schiller & Asmus, Inc., Yemasse, S.C., U.S.A.; Cuisinarts, Inc., Greenwich, Conn., U.S.A.; KitchenAid, Inc., Troy, Ohio, U.S.A.; Oster, Milwaukee, Wis., U.S.A.

Typesetting by G. Beard and Son Ltd., Brighton, Sussex, England
Printed and bound by Brepols S.A., Turnhout, Belgium